Spotlight on

Alain Anderton

Spotlight on Economics and Society

A skills-based approach

Pitman

PITMAN PUBLISHING LIMITED
128 Long Acre, London WC2E 9AN

A Longman Group Company

© Alain Anderton 1986

First published in Great Britain 1986

British Library Cataloguing in Publication Data
Anderton, A. G.
  Spotlight on economics and society.
  1. Great Britain—Economic conditions—1945–
  I. Title
  330.941'0858   HC256.6

  ISBN 0-273-02319-5

Printed in Great Britain at The Bath Press, Avon

Contents

vii

Preface

Spotlight on Economics and Society has been written for the young person in the last years at school or beginning a college course. The book sets out to help young people understand the way in which the country earns its living and to understand their own role as consumers, producers and citizens. It should be helpful to pupils on all prevocational courses, particularly those mounted as part of CPVE and TVEI courses, as well as to pupils studying economics as a single subject or as a component in a social studies course.

Spotlight on Economics and Society is conventional in layout, with each chapter dealing with a recognizable aspect of the subject. Straightforward exercises that relate to the text are interspersed throughout. Each chapter concludes with a summary and more substantial tasks aimed at extending the students' skills in that area. Each task is free standing and teachers and lecturers need to choose which of the exercises would be most appropriate for the development of their students. There is a wide range of tasks for teachers to develop skills such as literacy, numeracy, communication, and decision making.

I would like to thank Ronald Bramham for commenting on the draft of the book, Sheila Collins and Margaret Hope for typing the manuscript and to those at Pitman who helped produce the book.

Alain Anderton

Acknowledgements

The authors and publishers would like to thank the following for permission to reproduce copyright material:

Acorn Computers Ltd.;
Austin Rover Group/British Leyland;

BBC;
British Gas;

Co-operative Bank;

Frank Innes Estate Agents;

National Westminster Bank plc;
Nationwide;

Post Office;
Prime Computers Ltd.;

Royal Insurance;

Stock Exchange;

Tesco Stores Ltd.

1 Economics—a way of thinking

What is economics?

'Economics—that's something to do with money isn't it?' Money is certainly an important part of economics, but it is only one part. The reason why money is important in an economy is that it can buy **real** goods and services—like motorbikes, or a holiday in Spain, or a magazine, or make-up—both now and in the future. It is these real goods and services and how they are allocated which form the basis of the study of economics.

Everybody is caught up in the economic system, because everybody faces the same basic **economic problem**. The problem starts with man's **infinite wants**. There seems to be no limit to how much an individual wants. Even in the richest society in the world today—the United States of America—everybody, even multi-millionaires, wants to have more goods and services. But, the world's economy cannot provide everything that is wanted. **Resources** are **scarce**. There are only so many workers, so many machines, so many raw materials, available at a point in time. Because resources are scarce, they have to be allocated between people, between firms, between countries. Economics is devoted to the study of how the **allocation of resources** takes place.

Exercise

In five minutes, try to list as many items as you would like to have if everything were free. Could you go on adding to your list? What does this prove about wants?

Resource allocation

There are two main ways in which resources are allocated in the world today. The first is through the **market mechanism**. A market is where buyers and sellers meet and exchange. In a local market, stallholders sell or **supply** their goods to housewives who want to buy or **demand** vegetables. In the labour market, workers supply their services to employers who demand labour. In a market, it is the **price** of products which ensures the allocation of resources. When too many products are produced for sale and consumers won't buy them (i.e. supply is greater than demand), prices fall—as in the January sales. When too few products are produced and consumers want to buy more (i.e. demand is greater than supply), prices tend to go up.

The second main way in which resources are allocated is through the **state**. A government will produce goods and services and distribute them to its citizens. In Britain, for instance, this is what happens with the National Health Service (NHS): people who need medical care can get it free of charge. Resources still have to be allocated. The NHS cannot afford to spend as much as it would like to. So there are waiting lists for some operations, hospitals do not always have the latest equipment, and doctors cannot afford to spend as much time with their patients as they would like.

2 *Exercise*

Have you ever bought anything in a sale or at a reduced price? What was it? Why do you think that the price of the item was reduced? Use the terms 'demand' and 'supply' in your answer.

Choices

Allocation implies **choice**. If there is only a limited number of goods and services to be distributed, then choices have to be made about the distribution of those resources. At an individual level, choices have to be made because resources are scarce. Will you buy a chocolate bar or a magazine? Will you become a plumber or an electrician? At national level, governments have to choose too. Government spending cuts are the result of choices that government has made about how to allocate its resources.

Choices are often hard to make, because one course of action necessitates giving up something else. If you only have 20p to spend, then either you can buy a chocolate bar or a magazine, but not both. If you buy the chocolate bar, you can't buy the magazine. In economics, it is said that the **opportunity cost** of that chocolate bar is a magazine. The opportunity cost of a chocolate bar is the benefit to be gained from the next most desirable alternative which has to be given up in order to be able to get the chocolate bar.

Exercise

What is your average weekly income? How, on average, do you spend that money? What is the opportunity cost of £1 of that expenditure (i.e. what would you most like to spend £1 on if you couldn't spend £1 on some of the products you buy at the moment)?

Efficiency

Because resources are scarce and because choices are always difficult to make, it is essential that the economy be as efficient as possible. There are a number of different ways in which economists judge whether or not **economic efficiency** is present. One way of judging is to see whether or not goods and services are produced at lowest cost. If Japan, for instance, can produce a car for half the cost of a British car, then it is likely that British car manufacturers are inefficient. Another aspect is whether or not consumers are able to buy goods and services at lowest prices.

If producers are wasting large sums of money on advertising or simply making excessive profits, then economic inefficiency is present. Yet another aspect is the quality and availability of goods and services. For instance, is the economy producing as good quality cars as it can and do they incorporate the latest technology?

Making the best or most efficient use of scarce resources from an individual level right through to an international level should be the aim of all economic decision-makers. This and the implications of the basic economic problem of a scarcity of resources, form the subject matter of the rest of this book.

3

Exercise

Is your school or college run efficiently? Are there any ways in which you think it could be run more cheaply and provide the same service, or provide a better service, with the money it receives?

Important points to keep in mind

1. **Man's wants are infinite.**
2. **But resources are scarce.**
3. **So everybody has to make choices.**
4. **Every economic choice has an economic cost—the opportunity cost of that cause of action.**
5. **Resources can be allocated either through the free market mechanism or by the state.**
6. **It is desirable that resources be allocated in as efficient a way as possible.**

TASK

If you had £100 to spend, what would you choose to buy if you could only spend the money on clothes or hi-fi equipment? Would you prefer to spend all or part of that £100 on other goods? Explain why this is an example of choice and the allocation of resources.

Shroud-waving for a slice of the NHS cake

By Andrew Veitch

DOCTORS wanting a slice of the shrinking health budget have to be aware of one basic principle: choices between items as different as a couple of new hip joints or a new hospital chaplain finally come down to personal feeling — the greater the emotional appeal of a proposal, the better its chances.

The heart surgeons at Guy's Hospital in London are using it to great effect in their fight to keep their theatres open.

The proposition that 100 or more patients will die — as they surely will — if Guy's open heart unit closes for a couple of months because the local health authority is short of a few pounds is guaranteed to stir the emotions. It's called shroud-waving in the trade.

The Guy's unit is funded by Lewisham and North Southwark district health authority. The authority, in common with every other in the country, had been told by health ministers to improve services for the elderly, the mentally ill, and the mentally handicapped.

Under a 10-year plan, the authority plans to increase expenditure on services for the mentally ill from £4.6 million a year now to £11.5 million in 1984. Expenditure on services for the mentally handicapped will rise from £2.6 million to £4.8 million. And expenditure on the elderly will increase from £8.6 to £10.6 million.

Community homes will be built for patients now incarcerated in the old long-stay mental hopsitals — six to a home, with staff to treat them.

However, the Government will give Lewisham no more money for these services.

To cope with this, Lewisham is to close three of its five hospitals — Hither Green, New Cross, and Sydenham children's hospital — and concentrate resources on Guy's and Lewisham hospitals. But it cannot allow one unit to overspend by £272,000, for to do so would encourage other specialist units to use the same tactics.

If heart surgery is closed for a couple of months the authority can make major savings on nurses' salaries, drugs, oxygen, and equipment — artificial heart valves cost £1,000 each.

(*The Guardian*, 28 February 1985)

TASKS

1. What is meant by 'choice' in economics?

2. Give **two** examples of the sort of choice that a hospital might have to make.

3. What choices are being faced by Lewisham and North Southwark district health authority?

4. Why does Lewisham have to make these choices?
   Use the phrase 'scarce resources' in your answer.

5. Why should Lewisham want to close Guy's open heart unit?

6. What will be the cost of closing this unit?

7. What is the government's ten-year plan for the health service?

8. Do you think the government is right in allocating scarce resources in the health service according to this plan?

Acorn introduces B Plus model

By Jason Crisp

ACORN, the home-computer group, launched an enhanced version of the BBC Micro yesterday. The model, the BBC B Plus, costs £499.

It has received a cool reception from some leading retail chains. They say it is too expensive. The model has a larger memory and better facilities than the standard BBC Micro, which has been Acorn's leading product line.

W. H. Smith and Boots have not decided whether to stock the machine. Mr Peter Frost, Boots computer buyer, said it was too costly. Boots would be more sympathetic if it cost £450.

At £499 the B Plus looks expensive compared with products from other companies such as Sinclair Research, Commodore and Atari which have the same or more memory. Apart from the enhancements, the BBC Micro is also an older machine than those offered by rivals.

Acorn says the BBC Micro's reliability, the availability of good software and the fact it can be expanded will ensure it remains competitive. UK home-computer market weakness, however, is likely to put strong pressure on prices.

(*Financial Times*, 1 May 1985)

TASKS

1. What does Acorn produce?
2. According to the article, what new product has Acorn launched?
3. What makes the 'BBC B Plus' better than the standard BBC Micro?
4. Name two 'leading retail chains' which sell computers.
5. According to the article, why have W. H. Smith and Boots not decided whether to sell the BBC B Plus?
6. What would happen to demand for the BBC B Plus if it were priced at £450?
7. Explain why demand for the B Plus is likely to be low at a price of £499.
8. Why do you think Acorn has decided to set such a high price for its new computer?
9. Why do you think the price of the B Plus is likely to fall from its initial price of £499?

5

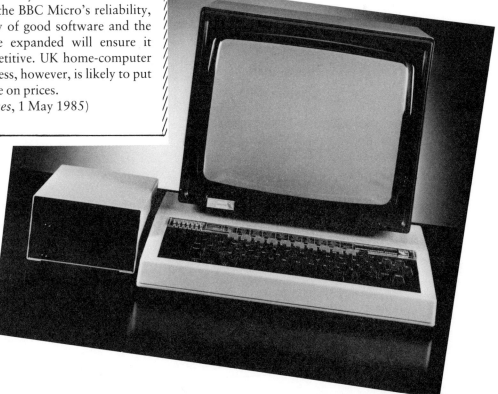

Bus privatisation studies show runaway costs

Geoffrey Andrews

THE Government's claims that privatisation of bus services will save £200 million have been dealt a severe blow by a report prepared for a Conservative-controlled council.

The study, for the Hertfordshire council, suggests that privatisation will cost £3 for every pound saved in a typical county.

The Hertfordshire study anticipated that within the next two years changes in the transport supplementary grant would result in something like a cut of £1 million from the amount the county would have available to support its bus services, now £5 million a year.

The study set out to find the best ways to implement the changes, the options, and the knock-on effect in areas like education, social services and employment.

The principal financial conclusion of the study is that to save £1 million on bus services the county would have to find economies on public services amounting to over £2.4 million. This is largely because of the cost of providing extra contract coaches for schoolchildren.

The costs of extra ambulance services, social service transport, and works buses would add a further £500,000. Revenue losses would be £1.3 million.

The changes would mean the withdrawal of more than 25 routes and cuts on more than 20 others—almost 40 per cent of all the routes in the county. Many of the routes affected would be lightly used, but nevertheless vital, rural services. Concentrating the cuts in the towns would have made the balance sheet even more unfavourable.

About 3.5 million passenger trips would no longer be made, 750,000 of them by elderly people using concessionary tickets.

This shrunken network would require a 13 per cent staff cut, with over 100 redundancies.

Even with the extra contract coaches a large number of children who do not qualify for special transport would be deprived of a bus service to school.

Although the report does not put a figure on the cost of the extra accidents it says: 'In many cases these necessary trips to school will be made on foot, by bicycle or by moped or motorcycle, all of which have road safety implications.'

(*The Guardian*, 3 December 1984)

TASKS

1 What is meant by 'privatisation'?

2 The government wants to cut the subsidy which Hertfordshire gives for bus services which are unprofitable. How much money does Hertfordshire provide to run its bus services at the moment? By how much does Hertfordshire think this will be cut?

3 A cut in subsidies for buses would mean fewer buses.
   a How many routes would be closed?
   b How many routes would see a reduction in services?
   c What would be the effect on the number of trips made by passengers?
   d How many workers would get the sack?

4 What would be the effect of this cut in subsidies on
   a the education services?
   b the health service?
   c the social services?
   d local businesses in the area?

5 Why should a cut in bus subsidies lead to more traffic accidents?

6 Would a £1 million cut in bus subsidies lead to a more efficient use of resources in Hertfordshire? To answer this, compare the current situation, where taxpayers have to pay £1 million in taxes to pay for bus subsidies, with the possible situation where bus subsidies are cut by £1 million but bus services are also cut.

2 Budgeting

Why budget?

'Jane, lend me 80p will you? I'm really hungry and I haven't got any money left this week. I just don't know where it all goes. I'll pay you back on Saturday. Honest!'

Are you like this? Do you find it difficult to make ends meet? Are you always running out of money before you get your next pocket money or wage packet? Here, you are experiencing the basic **economic problem**—that your wants are always greater than the resources available to you.

Exercise

When was the last time you ran out of money? Is this a regular feature of your life?

What is a budget?

Lurching from week to week, never quite knowing whether or not you are going to have enough money to get by, is not a sensible way of managing your money. A good idea is to draw up a **budget**. A budget shows you what you spend your money on and whether or not you can afford that expenditure. You can also compare what you have spent with your own targets and see where you're overspending or underspending. This will tell you which shops to avoid each week!

Making a budget

The first stage in making a budget is to draw up a list of your regular sources of income. We'll assume that you are still at school or college. Your income might look like this:

Allowance from Dad	£3.00
Saturday job	£10.00
Cleaning the car	£1.50
Total weekly income	£14.50

Now you have to draw up a list of your weekly expenditure. It must be no more than your income, or else you will get deeper and deeper into debt—something to be avoided. You might decide to spend it like this:

Food	£1.00
Clothes	£5.00
Records	£2.00
Big purchases	£6.50
Total	£14.50

'Big purchases' refer to those which you make only once in a while and are normally fairly expensive items, such as Christmas presents or going to a rock concert.

Every week, you now keep a record of your income and your expenditure. An actual week's budget might look like this:

Expenditure		Income	
Food:		**Allowance**	£3.00
5 Mars Bars	£0.85		
Packet of chips	£0.30		
Clothes:		**Saturday job**	£10.00
Blouse	£7.99		
Records:			
Duran Duran	£4.99	**Cleaning the car**	£1.50
Big purchases:			
None	£0.00		
Saving	£0.37		
	£14.50		£14.50

This week, you spent more on food, clothes and records than you planned, but didn't spend anything on big purchases. The result was that you were able to save 37p overall. You can see that you cannot afford to buy clothes and records every week if you are to keep within your planned budget. You are also eating too much—you cannot afford to buy five Mars Bars and a packet of chips a week. Budgeting and keeping a record of your income and expenditure helps you spend wisely and prevents you sliding into debt without understanding where you are overspending. It also helps you make choices. It's all too easy to spend money on the spur of the moment and then have regrets because you would have really preferred to spend your money in another way. Keeping a budget makes you realize that if you overspend on one item, it means that you now can't afford to buy something else.

Exercise

Do you keep a budget? If yes, describe it. If no, why don't you and wouldn't it be a good idea if you did? Do you think that

8

making a budget will be more or less important when you get a job than now?

Saving

Everybody saves—saving simply means that money is not spent immediately. Each week, you are most unlikely to spend exactly what you earn. You will either underspend, and thus add to your savings, or you will overspend and have to finance that either by drawing on your savings or borrowing the money. The ways in which you can borrow money will be discussed in the next chapter. In the rest of this chapter, we will concentrate on saving.

9

There are a number of reasons why you might want to save. Firstly, you might want to put away money now to spend in the future. Most people, for instance, spend more at Christmas time than at other times of the year, so they save up for it. Secondly, you might want to buy a very large item—like a motorbike or a car—which you can't afford with just one week's income. Thirdly, you might want to save up for a rainy day, when the car goes wrong, or the washing machine breaks down, or you lose your job. It's handy to have savings put by to deal with these emergencies. Fourthly, you might want to see your money grow. Interest is usually given on savings and at the end of the year you will be a richer person than at the start.

Exercise

Do you save on a regular basis? Why do you save money?

Ways of saving

There are a variety of ways in which you could save your money. These include:

(1)   In a tin, under the mattress, behind the flower pot. This is fine for small sums of money, where you want instant access to your savings. So, it's good for those small sums you might have left over at the end of the week. But it's not a very safe way to save. Having large sums of money around the house is an open invitation to burglars. You also don't earn interest on your savings.

(2)   In a bank deposit account or a building society account. These will give you interest on your savings. There are a number of different types of account available and it's worth shopping around between banks and building societies to see which gives you the highest rate of interest. Generally speaking, the more money you have saved and the more awkward it is to withdraw your money, the higher the rate of interest. In 1985, for instance, the building societies were offering an extra $1\frac{1}{2}\%$ on top of their normal rate to savers who saved at least £500 and who had to give 28 days' notice if they wanted to get their money out. Interest is paid **net** of tax—which means that building societies and banks pay income tax owed on the interest on your behalf to the

government. If you don't pay income tax, you won't be able to claim this money back, so you might be better off with a saving scheme which gives you a higher **gross** rate of interest—where gross means that no income tax has been deducted.

(3)   At the Post Office. The Post Office runs a variety of saving schemes including an Investment Account, National Savings Certificates and Premium Bonds. Leaflets are available from any Post Office explaining these schemes. Most are designed for the longer-term saver who wants to put away for years rather than days or weeks.

(4)   Assurance. This is a very long-term form of regular saving, normally for 25 years. Your parents may have taken out an assurance policy on your behalf when you were young, saving a little each week so that you could have a few hundred pounds on, say, your 21st birthday. Before taking out assurance, make sure that you can afford to set aside money each week or month and that the company offering the assurance policy has done well in the past.

Exercise

Where do you save? Do you think this is the best place for you to save at the moment? Why, or why not?

Important points to keep in mind

1. **A budget indicates how you plan to spend your income and where your income comes from.**

2. **Keeping a regular account of your income and expenditure will help you to see how you are spending your money according to your budget plans.**

3. **You will certainly save money at some time. You might save to buy a large item in the future, as a precaution against unexpected bills or to earn interest.**

4. **There is a variety of ways in which you can save including a 'piggy bank' at home, in a bank or building society, at the Post Office or with an assurance company.**

Outline budget

Expenditure £	Income £
Food	Pocket money
Housing	Wage
Electricity/ Gas/Water	
Transport	Supplementary benefit
Clothes	
Insurance	Borrowing
Entertainment	
Loan repayments	Other
Saving	
Other	
Total _____	Total _____

1 Start by drawing up a budget for yourself right now, showing a typical week's spending and income.

2 Imagine you have left school or college and are on the YTS. Find out how much you would be paid. Assume you have no other income and are still living at home with your parents. It's costing you £5.20 a week in bus fares to get to and from work. You have borrowed £60 from your dad to buy some suitable clothes for work and you're paying him back at a rate of £2 a week. You're also giving something to your mum for food (you have to decide how much is a fair amount to give).

3 You're unemployed, living in a flat with three other friends. You get £25 a week supplementary benefit. The Department of Health and Social Security is paying your share of the rent on top of that. You occasionally help out at a local pub and get an average of £4 a week as a result.

4 You're married, no children. Both you and your spouse (husband or wife) have regular jobs bringing in a total of £150 a week. You're renting a furnished flat for £50 a week. You bought a colour TV and are still paying back £7.50 a week on it. You're trying to save up for a house and you aim to save £25 a week. Bus fares come to £14.50 a week for both of you. You would like a holiday in Spain this summer.

TASK

From the outline, budget for each of the four situations described above; completing the budget as if you were the person involved. Only include those categories of expenditure and income which would apply in your situation. So if you were unemployed, for instance, you would possibly miss out 'Pocket money' and 'wage'.

Now imagine that your income in each of these situations changed. What would you choose to spend your money on if your income went **up** by 10%? What would you decide to cut down on if your income **fell** by 10%?

Nationwide

for regular savings

Subscription Shares

Net	Gross Equivalent	Minimum Subscription	Maximum Subscription
9.25%	**13.21%**	**£1**	**£400** (Joint Account)

Extra interest for regular savings

Regular saving is ideal for saving for a target like a holiday, car, or perhaps the deposit on a house. You can start a Subscription Share Account with monthly savings from £1 to £200 (£400 in a joint account).
You decide how much you want to save, and you can stop saving whenever you like. You must save 12 equal payments each year, but you can increase your subscription at any time.

Withdrawals
You can make one withdrawal in each calendar year without losing the extra interest. You can withdraw the full amount whenever you like. If you decide to stop saving regularly but still want to keep your account open, it can be converted to a Share Account or FlexAccount so that you can continue to add to it or withdraw from it.

How your savings grow

PERIOD (Years)	MONTHLY SUBSCRIPTIONS							
	£5	£10	£20	£25	£50	£100	£200	£400*
	£	£	£	£	£	£	£	£
1	63	126	252	315	630	1260	2520	5040
2	132	264	527	659	1318	2637	5273	10547
3	207	414	828	1035	2070	4141	8281	16562
4	289	578	1157	1446	2892	5784	11567	23135
5	379	758	1516	1895	3789	7579	15157	30315
6	477	954	1908	2385	4770	9540	19080	38159
7	584	1168	2336	2920	5841	11682	23364	46729
8	701	1402	2804	3505	7011	14023	28046	56092
9	828	1658	3316	4145	8290	16580	33160	66320
10	968	1937	3874	4843	9686	19373	38747	77495

This table assumes that the rate of interest continues at 9.25%.

The balances shown for each year-end are to the nearest pound and may vary depending on the date of opening the account.

*Monthly subscriptions of more than £200 apply only to joint accounts.

P66D April 85

Source: Nationwide Building Society

TASK

1. What is the rate of interest after income has been paid on the account?

2. The account is described as a 'regular saving' account. What does this mean?

3. How much do you have to save in the account?

4. How easy is it to withdraw money from the account?

5. How much would a person have saved including interest if that person saves
   - £20 a month for 2 years
   - £100 a month for 3 years
   - £15 a month for 8 years?

6. Why might a person want to save on a regular basis?

7. Give **two** reasons why saving regularly with the Nationwide would help you to buy a first house.

8. If you had just left school and were starting a YTS job, do you think it would be a good idea to open a subscription account? Explain your answer carefully.

9. Saving involves choice. If **you** had £2 a week spare, what would you have to give up if you decided to save it?

SECOND GENERATION SAVING

ON LINE is the 'Second Generation Saving System', designed to meet the needs of modern, sophisticated young people under the age of 19.

ON LINE helps you to save by giving you interest on your money.

And when you want to spend some of your hard-earned savings, ON LINE gives you a special purchasing facility over a wide range of goods.

These items have been specially selected with you in mind – and range from sports goods to a home computer, from cameras to a personal stereo.

ON LINE SAVING

£5 is enough to open an ON LINE account. Of this, £3 is credited to your account to start you off, and the remaining £2 goes towards your stylish ON LINE wallet.

The wallet contains your slim ON LINE calculator. The memory function stores information even when the unit is switched off, allowing you to recall your current balance at the touch of a key.

Also included in the wallet is a pen, your ON LINE card, which carries your signature and personal Codeholder Number, and a space for your paying-in book (posted separately).

ON LINE savers also receive the Codeholders' Manual and a file for six-monthly account statements issued every July and January.

Interest at the applicable rate and calculated on a daily basis is normally credited to the account in June and December automatically. Rates available in branches.

All ON LINE account holders will regularly receive a glossy ON LINE magazine containing lots of interesting articles, advice on money matters, news and competitions.

ON LINE SPENDING

When you open your ON LINE account, you will receive the exclusive ON LINE Handbook containing details of the specially selected items available to Codeholders.

You can dial a special telephone number and order a particular item using the Codeholder Number from your ON LINE card.

Providing there are sufficient funds in the account, the item will automatically be despatched to you.

RUNNING YOUR ACCOUNT

You can pay into your ON LINE account at any of the 3,200 NatWest branches across the country. Of course, should you wish, you may withdraw cash from your branch and, provided seven day's notice is given, interest will not be lost on the sum withdrawn.

May we remind you that cash credited to your account earns interest from the day it reaches the account. This will generally be three working days later if paid in at a branch other than the account holding branch.

If cheques are paid in, interest starts to accrue on the new balance from the day the cheques are 'cleared'. This too is generally three working days after being paid in.

You can become an ON LINE Codeholder at the stroke of a pen. Simply fill in the form on the reverse of this leaflet and take it to the branch of NatWest where you would like to have the account held.

Source: National Westminster Bank

13

TASK

1 What, according to the leaflet, are the advantages of opening an 'On Line' account with National Westminster Bank?

2 How much will it cost you to open an account?

3 How do you think this way of saving compares with, for instance, accounts at other banks, building societies or at the Post Office?

4 NatWest are unlikely to make a profit on a new On Line account for quite a while. Why is this so? Why are they prepared, then, to offer this account to young people?

Ernie's big share out

NOW – AN EVEN BETTER CHANCE OF WINNING

November 1984 saw the start of a new deal from ERNIE, with more prizes and more prize money. Not only is there an extra £1 million to be paid out every month, but every bond-holder has more chance of winning.

This is what new-look Premium Bonds offer each and every month:

- £10,500,000 worth of prizes.
- Over 150,000 prize-winners.

The number of prizes every month has gone up by something like 50,000. So with half as many prizes again, you've got a chance of winning more prizes more often.

And every month somebody wins the £250,000 jackpot prize.

Every week somebody like you has the thrill of receiving a letter from ERNIE letting them know they have won £100,000 or £50,000 or perhaps £25,000.

Everyone has a dream – a new car, a better house, the holiday of a lifetime. Maybe yours will come true with a little bit of help from ERNIE.

ERNIE'S BIG SHARE-OUT

Top monthly jackpot

£250,000

Weekly jackpot prizes

1 prize of £100,000
1 prize of £50,000
1 prize of £25,000

Other monthly prizes

5 prizes of £10,000
25 prizes of £5,000
Over 150,000 prizes from £1,000 to £50.

Your bond could win any of ERNIE'S prizes shown above once it has been held for three calendar months following the month of purchase. Each £1 bond unit has a separate chance of being drawn for a prize in each and every draw.

Tax-free prizes

All ERNIE's prizes are completely free of U.K. Income Tax and Capital Gains Tax. So **every** penny of prize money is yours to enjoy.

How you know you're a winner

When you win a prize, the Bonds and Stock Office will write to you with the good news at the last address you gave them.

If you change your address or name, please let the Bonds and Stock Office know as soon as possible. Don't risk becoming a winner who can't be traced. See the back of this leaflet for details.

Who can buy?

Any person over 16 can buy bonds – the application form must be signed by the purchaser.

Anyone under 16 can have bonds bought for them by parents, legally appointed guardians or grandparents. Full details are on the prospectus/application form. (A bond cannot be held in the names of more than one person.)

Buy from £5 to £10,000

Bonds are sold in multiples of £5, giving you five separate chances of a prize in every draw. You can hold up to £10,000 worth. Remember, the more bonds you have, the greater the chances of winning.

Where to buy

Premium Bonds can be bought at post offices and banks. Bonds of £5 and £10 value are handed over the counter, and those over £10 are sent to the holder from the Bonds and Stock Office.

Cashing in

You can get your money back by completing a repayment form obtainable at any post office and sending it together with the bonds to the Bonds and Stock Office.

Now – an extra £1 million of prizes every month!

Source: Department of National Savings, London

TASK

1 A Premium Bond is a form of saving. Explain how you can buy premium bonds.

2 When you save money, you normally expect to earn interest. What do you get instead of interest with Premium Bonds?

3 The government pays about 5% of all monies saved in Premium Bonds to holders for the use of their savings. If you had the choice to invest your savings in a building society account earning 10% interest OR betting for a year on the football pools OR buying Premium Bonds, which would you choose? Explain your answer carefully.

3 Shopping

Spending your money

At the moment, you probably don't have much money to spend. You may wonder how people spend £50 or £100 or more a week. But in ten years' time, £50 or £100 a week to spend may seem very little. By then you are likely to have commitments—a husband or wife to look after, children, possibly a large mortgage on the house you are buying. Obviously you will want to get the best value for money. How can you do this? How can you make your money go farther?

Budgeting

The first step in becoming a wise spender is to draw up a budget. You only have a limited amount of money to spend each week or each month. A large proportion of that may well go on fixed items of expenditure, like the rent or mortgage, rates (a tax on your house), electricity, gas and telephone bills, insurance payments, bus and rail fares or a car, repayments on loans, and so on. That leaves you only a relatively small amount of money to spend on food, clothes or entertainment. It's very easy to be tempted to buy more than you can really afford in the local supermarket, or in your favourite clothes shop. A budget will tell you how much you can spend without getting into financial difficulties. So budget wisely and keep to your budget.

Value for money

What should you be looking for when you want value for money in a purchase? There are a number of important considerations, including:

(1) *Suitability for the purpose*   Is what you bought what you really needed in the first place? For instance, you may decide that you need a new pair of shoes for work. These shoes should be practical and hard wearing. When you go to the shops, you see a beautiful pair of shoes in the latest fashion style. They're about the price you wanted to pay. The only problem is that they're not very practical and you don't think they're going to last very long either. Still, they are so fashionable that you decide to buy them all the same. Obviously, you haven't got value for money because you wanted to buy one thing and ended up buying something different. The shoes you bought were not suitable for your purpose.

(2) *Price*   The price of the products you buy should be as low as possible. This means being prepared to shop around. It's not

important if you pay 1p more for your favourite chocolate bar, but shopping around for something like a washing machine costing hundreds of pounds can save you a great deal of money.

(3)   *Quality*   The quality of products varies enormously. It's by no means always true that the more you pay for something, the better its quality. The price you pay for a product reflects the profit margin that the shop and the manufacturer make, the cost of advertising and selling, and the cost of production as well as the quality of an item. So, it's up to you to find out and decide what is best quality. Later on in this chapter we will be telling you about where you might find out about quality of products.

(4)   *After-sales service*   Particularly for large purchases, such as televisions or washing machines, it is important to consider after-sales service. To start with, can you take the product back if things go wrong? Is there a guarantee? How easy will it be to get the product repaired in ten years' time? With clothes, always look at the washing label: think carefully about buying anything which says 'dry clean only'—it will cost you far more to clean these clothes than if you can wash them by hand or in a machine.

Exercise

Have you ever bought something which you later regretted buying? What was it? Why did you regret buying it? What is good value for money in your opinion, and why or why not?

Where to shop

In order to get value for money, it's important to choose carefully where you shop. Take food, for instance. How do you decide where to buy food? Supermarkets have been the fastest growing type of food shop over the past 30 years. They provide a wide range of goods at cheap prices and, as a result, have come to replace the small local shop as the main supplier of groceries in Britain. Many people go for a 'weekly shop' to one supermarket— they don't shop around for the cheapest price on every item they buy. This makes sense if saving a few extra pence is not worth hours of extra shopping. It doesn't make sense if you're on a limited income—if you're unemployed for instance—and every penny you spend is important.

When you're in a supermarket, shop around for the best value. There may be a special offer on a brand. Own brands (products sold under the name of the supermarkets) are usually excellent value. Look out too for 'generics', which are products bought by the supermarket from whichever manufacturer is able to offer the cheapest price at the time. They are then put into plain packaging and sold under the supermarket's name. They are different from own brands because they are normally cheaper and also because the product inside the package may vary from month to month—

Source:
Tesco Stores Ltd.

one month, the supermarket may have bought cornflakes from one company, the next month it may be from another company.

Some small supermarkets, such as Kwiksave, carry a very limited range of products—normally about 500—and keep costs down by not pricing each product individually and stacking shelves using the original manufacturers' cartons. The result is rock bottom prices.

You're likely to buy some items from the small local shop too. The local shop is convenient: no long queues at check-out tills, and they are likely to be within walking distance. Packaged products are likely to be more expensive than at the local supermarket. The corner shop can't buy in big enough quantities to get the sort of discounts from the manufacturers that supermarkets can get. Fruit and vegetables, however, may well be cheaper than at the supermarket.

Exercise

What food shops does your family shop at? Is there any single shop from which most of the family's food is purchased? What is it's name? Why does your family shop at these shops rather than others?

Non-food shopping

What about non-food items? As with food, more and more money is being spent in large chain shops, such as Marks and Spencer's, Boots, W. H. Smith's, Curry's, MFI or B & Q. Large chains can buy high-quality products at discount prices from manufacturers and pass on the savings to their customers. It's worth shopping around these big high street shops to get best value for money on expensive items.

Many consumers buy goods from large mail-order catalogues—like Kays or Brian Mills. This is a very convenient way of shopping, especially if you have a very demanding job or you can't face taking the family to town on a shopping trip. Some items in the mail-order catalogues are good value for money, but for the most part you should expect to pay a little more than the cheapest prices in shops for the privilege of shopping at home.

Whatever your income, you may buy from jumble sales, auctions or second-hand shops. Genuine bargains are available—and many people enjoy picking through what's on sale to find these. But for every bargain, there are likely to be many poor-quality items. Being choosy is all important. If you succeed you can dress yourself and equip your house for next to nothing.

Exercise

Write down two items of clothing bought for you or by you recently. Where were they bought? Why were they bought in that particular shop or from that catalogue? Did they represent good value for money? Why, or why not?

Obtaining credit

Borrowing money can be both a good idea and a bad idea depending upon your circumstances. The advantages of buying on credit are that you don't have to wait to get the goods, you can take advantage of special offers and bargain prices, and because you find it so difficult to save, this is the only way you'll ever get expensive goods. The disadvantages are that you normally have to pay interest on the money you borrow and that if you don't repay your debts you can be taken to court, your possessions can be sold and you can generally get into deep trouble.

Whenever you're tempted to take out a loan, think about two things. Firstly, can I really afford the repayments? Secondly, is it the cheapest way of buying the item that I want? If you're unemployed, for instance, it would be silly to borrow large sums of money. Equally, it would be silly for most people to try and save enough money to buy a house outright—getting a mortgage (a loan on a house) is the only realistic way in which the average man in the street will ever be able to afford to buy a house.

There are a number of different ways in which money can be borrowed. A **mortgage** is a loan to buy a house or other property. Most mortgages are given by building societies but you can also get them from banks and more rarely from assurance companies. The great advantage of a mortgage is that it is a very cheap form of borrowing. Not only are interest rates on mortgages relatively low, but you can also get tax relief on the interest you pay. What this means in practice is that you only pay two-thirds of the interest you would have paid. The drawback is that you can't get a mortgage to buy a television or a car, so you can't take advantage of the very cheap rates of interest offered for these items.

19

Exercise

Would you consider taking out a mortgage when you start earning money? Why or why not? What do you think would influence your decision about how much you would want to borrow?

Bank loans

Probably the best form of borrowing for ordinary consumers is a **bank loan**, 'best' because interest rates are likely to be low compared to other forms of borrowing. If you want to borrow money from a bank, you are likely to be offered a personal loan. The bank lends you the money for your television, or car or family holiday or whatever you are thinking of buying. You have to pay back the money with interest in equal monthly instalments. You can decide over what period to pay back the money, but the normal terms are between 6 months and 5 years. Another type of bank loan is an overdraft. Here the bank allows you to overdraw on your bank current account—so you need a bank account for this.

Credit cards

A **credit card** is a very convenient way of paying for goods and services as well as being a way to borrow money. The main credit cards in Britain are Access and Visa. You apply for a credit card and if your application is successful, the credit card company will send you your credit card and give you a credit limit. This limit is the maximum amount you may borrow from the company. When you buy something with your credit card, the shop fills out a slip giving details of the purchase. You keep one copy for your records and the shop sends another copy to the credit card company. The credit card company pays the shop and then enters the item on your next monthly statement. When you receive this statement, you have two choices. Either you pay back all the money you owe, in which case no interest is charged, or you can pay back part of the money and borrow the rest. You will then pay interest on the money you borrow. As a means of payment, a credit card is very convenient because you don't have to worry about being short of cash, or carry much money about with you. As a way to borrow money, it is considerably more expensive than a bank loan.

Exercise

Would you consider ever applying for a credit card? What do you see as the advantages and disadvantages of having a credit card?

'Easy terms'

The most expensive way to borrow money is through hire purchase, loans from a specialist bank, or loans from a shop. 'Easy terms' usually means very high rates of interest and big repayments. These sorts of loans should be avoided if at all possible. The reason why interest rates are so high is that people who borrow in this way tend to be 'high-risk' borrowers, which means that there is a high risk that they will not pay back the money on time, if at all. So the lenders have to charge higher rates of interest to make up for the losses they suffer.

A word needs to be said about interest rates. If an advertisement says that the interest rate is 12%, this might not be true. There might be extra hidden charges, or the method of calculating the interest rate may not be the correct way. Fortunately, by law the true rate of interest must be stated on any advertisement or any contract: this is called the annual percentage rate or APR. The lower the APR, the lower the rate of interest. Always look at the APR when considering borrowing money, and do shop around for credit just as you shop around for goods and services.

Sources of advice and help

Consumers are able to get advice and help from a wide variety of sources. These include:

◆ Magazines and newspapers. Many magazines and newspapers carry the occasional consumer article. Look out for these. There are also specialist consumer magazines, the most useful probably being *Which?*, produced by the Consumers' Association. This is available by private subscription, but most public libraries carry copies which you can consult, free of charge. *Which?* carries articles on everything from cars to toothbrushes and often gives 'best buys'.

◆ The law. Consumers have strong legal rights. If you think that you have legal rights in a particular situation, go and see your local Trading Standards Department, run by your local authority. The Trading Standards Department may have an office in a local shopping centre called a 'Consumer Advice Centre'.

◆ Organizations. The Trading Standards Department and the Consumers' Association have already been mentioned. The Citizens Advice Bureau will give help and advice too.

Exercise Go to your local public library and ask for the latest copy of *Which?* magazine. Read it through and summarize one of the reports contained in it.

Important points to keep in mind

1 Never spend money without knowing you can really afford it. Having a budget and keeping to it is the best way to prevent this.

2 Make sure you always get value for money—look at price, quality, after-sales service and whether or not it's really what you need.

3 For most items, large chain stores usually offer best value for money, but you may pick up bargains at your local small shop, which is usually more convenient.

4 When finding out the cost of credit, always look for the APR. Only borrow money through hire purchase or other shop credit as a last resort because these loans are so expensive. A bank loan is usually the cheapest loan available.

5 Don't be afraid to get help or to claim your legal rights.

Domestic harmony

TASK

1 Did the daughter get value for money with her dress? Why?

2 Did the husband do the best thing in buying the car? Why?

3 What items have you bought in the past which you felt were not good value for money and why?

Shopping survey

Here are the results of a shopping survey taken in Fine Fare supermarket in Staffordshire in 1985.

Item: Automatic Washing Powder			
Brand name	*Size*	*Price (in pence)*	*Other information of importance*
Ariel	E3/930 g	99	
	E10/3.1 kg	258	
Persil	E3/930 g	89	*Competition to win*
	E10/3.1 kg	275	*£50,000 house*
Bold 3	E3/930 g	102	*Includes fabric conditioner*
	E10/3.1 kg	302	*Includes fabric conditioner*
Daz	E3/930 g	89	*20p off next purchase*
Automatic	E10/3.1 kg	262	*30p off next purchase*
Fine Fare	E3/903 g	67	*Supermarket own brand*
	E10/3.1 kg	209	*Supermarket own brand*
Fine Fare	E3/930 g	79	*Supermarket own brand*
Biological	E10/3.1 kg	229	*Supermarket own brand*
Yellow Label	4.5 kg	265	*Generic*

22

TASK 1

1 Calculate a **unit price** for each size and each different brand, e.g. calculate the price of each packet per kg of content.

2 What different features would you consider when deciding which soap powder gives good value for money?

3 Explain which soap powder gave best value for money in the survey.

TASK 2

Construct your own survey based upon the washing powder example above.

◆ Decide which product or products you would like to investigate—such as coffee, shampoo or baked beans.

◆ Construct a survey grid.

◆ Go to a local shop, preferably a large one which carries a wide range of products, and collect the data.

◆ Write up your findings, using method in Task 1.

Price survey

TASK

Calculate the cheapest brand or size per 100 g.

	Item	Size (g)	Price (pence)	Price per 100 g	Cheapest (tick)
1	Circle butter	250	60		
	Triangle butter	500	130		
	Square butter	1000	200		
2	Festo jam	250	50		
		500	80		
		1000	150		
3	Beast dog food	500	150		
		750	60		
		1500	115		
4	Kenya coffee	100	150		
	India coffee	200	360		
	Brazil coffee	500	600		
5	Delice soup	500	40		
	Yum soup	1000	90		
	Special soup	2000	200		

Which shop?

This is a group-based research project designed to help you understand value for money.

TASK

1 Draw up a list of items commonly bought by members of the group (such as a packet of crisps, a pair of socks, a particular margarine).

2 Take one of these items. Make a list of all the shops where it could be purchased in your locality.

3 Discuss the advantages and disadvantages of buying it from each shop (you need to take into consideration factors such as price, convenience, quality of service).

4 Repeat the exercise for another item.

24

SHOPPING AROUND

SINGER 247 SEWING MACHINE			**BLACK AND DECKER WM 300 WORKMATE**
	Freemans:	£79.95	
	Grattan:	£79.95	
	Kays:	£85.95	
	John Myers:	£85.95	
	Empire Stores:	£89.95	

TOWER HI-DOME PRESSURE COOKER

STAR WARS WATCH

Kays:	£13.99	Kays:	£19.99	Kays:	£29.50
John Myers:	£13.99	Littlewoods:	£19.99	Littlewoods:	£29.50
Empire Stores:	£14.99	John Myers:	£19.99	John Myers:	£29.50
Littlewoods:	£14.99	Grattan:	£22.50	Freemans:	£29.95
Freemans:	£16.99	Freemans:	£22.95	Empire Stores:	£31.99
		Empire Stores:	£23.99	Grattan:	£34.99

Shopping by the book

No longer the preserve of mums, aunts and next-door-neighbours, those home shopping catalogues are competing for everyone's money now. But do they offer a good deal in terms of price, fashion and choice? Actionwoman reports

Price probe
Catalogues may give their customers the three Cs of Credit, Convenience, and Choice, but they don't automatically offer a fourth—Cheapness.

Since, they have to be printed long before publication, their prices for some items may be quite different from those in the shops. This cuts both ways. When prices are rising the catalogues can look cheap, but when shops are cutting prices, prices in the catalogues may seem extra high.

You might well find better bargains in different catalogues. As the Shopping Around chart below shows, it's possible to save pounds by switching to a different catalogue for some goods.

Around 90 per cent of catalogue sales through agents are on credit, and in general that is interest-free—apart from very expensive items with long repayment periods. But the interest charges are built into the advertised prices, which can make them seem higher than those in the shops.

If you take the trouble to work out most shops' full credit prices, though, you might decide that the catalogue offers the best deal after all.

Source: Woman, 26 January 1985

TASK

1 Explain how big mail-order catalogues offer 'Convenience and Choice'.

2 What is meant by 'interest-free' credit?

3 Why is credit not really 'interest-free' in a mail-order catalogue?

4 Why are mail-order catalogue prices often higher than in the average street shop?

5 Is it worth 'shopping around' between catalogues? Why might this be difficult to do in practice?

6 Bring several mail-order catalogues to class. Draw up a list of **ten** standard items and then check on the price of these in each catalogue. Which catalogue offers best value for money overall?

Which method?

Co-operative Bank

25

VISA CARD

Also included in our range of lending services is the Co-operative Bank Visa Card for customers who prefer to make their purchases with a credit card. You can use your Visa Card at home and abroad wherever you see the international VISA sign—shops, hotels, restaurants, garages, travel agents, car hire and much more.

Provided that you do not exceed your credit limit and you repay the minimum amount each month (at least 5% of the statement total, or £5 whichever is the greater) you can buy what you want, when you want it and spread the cost over a period of months to suit your budget.

For further details please complete the coupon at the end of this leaflet, and hand it to your local branch or send it by post using the special Freepost envelope, remembering to write VISA Department in the space provided on the envelope.

Personal Loans

The current annual rate of charge for Personal Loans for sums above £1,000 over periods of between 18 months and 5 years is 22%, equivalent to an APR of **23.4%**.

The current annual rate of charge on Personal Loans for sums of £1,000 or less or loans repaid over periods of 12 months or less is 24%, equivalent to an APR of **25.7%**.

Co-operative Bank Visa Card

The current rates of interest are:

Monthly rate	2.00%
APR for purchases	26.8%
APR for cash advances*	27.2%

*Assumes the cash advance is taken 2 weeks before it appears on the statement.

A Co-operative Bank

PERSONAL LOAN

You could enjoy an immediate credit to your current account of any amount from £500 to £6,000 yours to spend however you wish.

What would help you to a better life-style? A change of car? New furniture for your home? A new video or hi-fi system? Perhaps something for your favourite hobby?

Whatever it is, the Co-operative Bank may be able to help you with a Personal Loan.

A Co-operative Bank Personal Loan means more cash in your account

If your loan application is agreed, the cash is transferred into your Current Account, leaving you free to shop wherever you like, with your own cheque book.

A Co-operative Bank Personal Loan gives you the freedom to shop around

Shopping around means you can look for the best value for money, so you are not necessarily tied to a particular supplier. With the cash in your account you can also take advantage of the very real savings to be found at 'Sales' time, on new household equipment or furnishings, for example, and you may also be able to obtain a cash discount on larger items.

Vantage gives you the pick of the High Street

Your Vantage Account gives you more choice. Menswear, ladies fashions, shoes, TV, audio and video, department stores, duty free at Gatwick and Heathrow airports.

Everything you need for family shopping in 1,000 different shops and stores. Vantage will help you cope with expensive times like holidays, back-to-school, birthdays, weddings, sale times – Vantage spreads the cost right through the year.

You can then snap up fast selling lines and buy them when you want to.

As a Vantage accountholder, you'll be the first to hear of special offers and to receive details of exclusive money saving schemes.

How your Vantage Account works

First you decide how much to pay every month – you can start from as little as £8.

As soon as you receive your Vantage card you will be able to buy goods up to 24 times the value of your monthly payment. For example:

| £ 8 a month gives £192 spending |
| £10 a month gives £240 spending |
| £15 a month gives £360 spending |

Vantage gives you credit all year round

Vantage will provide you with continuous credit. This means that as long as the total amount you have spent, including interest, remains within your credit limit and your payments are up to date, you will be able to continue using your Vantage card. You won't have to wait until you've cleared one purchase before making another.

Receiving your statement of Account

Regular Vantage statements will help you keep a check on your buying. They'll show the purchases and the monthly payments you will have made and any interest charged or earned and the amount you have available to spend.

Joint Accounts

To make family shopping even more convenient, you may choose to open a joint account with your partner or other adult member of your family at no extra cost. Your joint account entitles each of you to your own Vantage card.

Your monthly payments

Your monthly payments are made by standing order. The Vantage application form includes a special standing order form for you to complete when applying for your Vantage Account.

Interest rates

Interest rates may vary from time to time. The current rate is 2.3% per month (equivalent to an Annual Percentage Rate of **31.3%**).

Vantage earns interest as you save

At certain times of the year you may build up a credit balance on your Vantage Account. You will then earn interest at a competitive rate on this balance. This rate is currently 12% per annum.

How to apply for your Vantage Account

Simply fill in the attached application form and standing order and send them to us. Once your application has been approved you'll receive your Vantage card within a few days.

Instant Credit with Vantage – Certainly!

If you're in a hurry, Instant Credit is available at most shops and stores.

To apply for Instant Credit simply ask one of the sales staff. They will help you to complete the application form which gives you spending power straight away. This is subject to certain conditions, for instance you must have a current account.

The above information is applicable from 1st October 1982, until further notice.

TASK

1. What are the names of the three different ways of borrowing money described on pages 25–27?

2. Explain how you **borrow** money with each of these.

3. Explain how you can repay money you have borrowed for each of the three schemes.

4. Which is (a) the most expensive and (b) the cheapest way to borrow of the three schemes?

5. You want to borrow money to buy (a) clothes worth £200, (b) a video cassette recorder priced £300, (c) a car priced £2000. Which form of borrowing would you recommend for each of these three items and why?

6. Which of these ways of borrowing is the most flexible when it comes to shopping around for a best buy when buying, say, a hi-fi system?

Best buy

This is a group-based project to investigate a particular product and decide what might be a 'best buy'. It would help if you could read beforehand several reports on products in the consumer magazine *Which?* or *Good Housekeeping*.

TASK

1 Get together with approximately **five** other people in your class and choose a product which is commonly used by all members of the group. Examples might be baked beans, school bags, shoes, home computers or motorbikes. When making your decision, try to pick a product which has several different brands on the market and which you will be able to test in the classroom.

2 Draw up a list of product characteristics which you think are important to test when trying to decide which is a best buy. You will almost certainly want to consider, among other things, the price of the product, its functionality (e.g. how well a school bag carries books and other equipment, how well a pair of shoes provides protective covering for feet), and aesthetic appeal (how well the product looks). Other important points to consider might be durability, packaging and after-sales service.

3 Test a number of different brands of the same product. For instance, compare the school bags owned by everybody in the group.

4 Each person should then write a 500-page word report on the product disclosing:

◆ how the product was tested

◆ what were the results of the various tests and then giving a conclusion where you attempt to give a 'best buy'.

Apple survey

This is another group-based project, designed to help you understand how to investigate a particular product and to decide the 'best buy'.

TASK

1 Get together with approximately five other people in your class and, between the six of you, arrange to have available as many different types of apple for investigation. For instance, decide that one person in the group will be responsible for buying the apples, or each person in the group is responsible for bringing along a different type of apple. Only one apple of each variety is needed for the investigation. The place of purchase and the price per lb or kilo should be noted.

2 The next time you have a lesson, complete the following questionnaire about each apple:

1   Name of apple

2   Country of origin

3   Price per lb or kilo

4   Place of purchase

5   Visual appeal

6   Smell

7   Texture

8   Taste

9   Other comments

The first four questions in this questionnaire should be relatively easy to answer. For questions 5 and 6, keep each apple whole. Use words like 'rosy', 'dull', 'unappetising', 'red', 'strong', 'bruised', 'well shaped', 'blemished'. For questions 7 and 8, cut the apple up and each of the group should taste each apple. A 'blind test' (where each tester does does not know which apple he or she is eating) would be preferable. Use words like 'juicy', 'tough', 'bland', 'sour', 'acidic', 'chewy', 'soft', 'unpleasant', 'delicious', when recording your comments.

3 Now decide on a 'best' buy.

4 Write a 500-word report on the apples surveyed, the test conducted and the results and conclusions made.

4 Accommodation

30

Where to live

Have you ever wondered where you will be living in two years' time? Or in 10 years' time? Or in 50 years' time? What sort of place would you like to have? Would you like to live in a flat, a house, or country residence? Is it important for you to own your own house? This chapter is devoted to considering the alternatives available to you and their relative costs.

The alternatives available

There are two basic choices open to you when it comes to obtaining accommodation: either you can rent or you can buy a place of your own. Over half the houses in this country are now 'owner-occupied'—that is, owned by the people living there. Most people buy a house by saving up money for a deposit (usually at least 10% of the price of the house) and then borrowing the rest. A loan to buy a house is called a mortgage and most mortgages are given by building societies or banks. The money is then repaid over a long period of time, such as 25 years. In order to afford the repayments, you must have a job which brings in a reasonable wage. You certainly should not think of buying a house if you are unemployed or on a very low wage.

Buying

Buying a house is a complicated and often long drawn out process. The first step is to save up enough money to put down as a **deposit** on the house. You should aim to save part of that money with the bank or building society where you hope to get a mortgage because if mortgages are in short supply, it will give first preference to its own regular savers. Before you start saving in earnest, it is a good idea to go and see your bank or building society manager to see what he thinks about your prospects of buying a house. He will advise you on how much you need to save for a deposit and what is the likely size of the mortgage you can expect to raise. Having saved enough money, go back and see your manager to check again about the size and availability of a mortgage. Then, if the financial side is satisfactory, you can go and choose a house, a flat, a maisonette or whatever you want to buy. It takes an average of three months from making an offer on a house to finally completing the purchase. In this time, there are many legal and technical formalities to arrange. These may

include having the house surveyed to check that it is in good condition, hiring a solicitor to deal with the contract of sale, and arranging for a removal van to transport your furniture from your present home. Finally, contracts are exchanged and you can move into your own home.

Exercise

Would you like eventually to own your own house? Give reasons why or why not.

Renting

If you can't afford a home of your own or if you prefer to rent, a number of options are available to you. You may try to rent a house or flat from your local council. A council house is usually excellent value for money—so good that nearly all councils have long waiting lists for houses. Unless you are a priority case—a family, for instance, with a small baby living in privately rented accommodation which is not fit for human habitation—you may have to wait months or, more likely, years. So if you want a council house, put your name down on the waiting list as soon as possible.

To start with, you are likely to rent accommodation from a private landlord. Accommodation and landlords differ greatly. If you are a 17-year-old, you might consider going into 'digs': you hire a furnished room in somebody's house and your landlord or landlady, who lives in the rest of the house, normally provides at least breakfast and possibly an evening meal too. Or you may hire a 'bed-sit', a furnished room in a house where the landlord may or may not be living. You have to do your own cooking, so a gas or electric ring is usually provided. You will have to share facilities like toilets and bathrooms with the other occupants or bed-sits in the building. You could try and get a place in a hostel, such as the YMCA (Young Men's Christian Association). Here you hire a furnished room and are then able to enjoy the facilities of the hostel, such as kitchens and a living room. In all of these, there are bound to be rules and regulations: you certainly will have to be careful about the amount of noise you make; you are unlikely to be able to keep pets; you may have to be in by a certain time each evening; there may be restrictions about who you can have to visit you in your room.

Alternatively, you may choose to rent a flat or a house. Most people who do this are either married or living with somebody, or they share the flat or house with friends. There are likely to be fewer rules and regulations laid down by the landlord. On the other hand, you will be living with other people and they will expect certain standards of behaviour from you. So, you still wouldn't be able to do just as you pleased.

If you are single, don't forget the advantages of living at home with Mum and Dad. Not only is it likely to cost you less than renting a place of your own, but you'll also be able to take advantage of many 'free' services provided by them—things like having meals cooked, washing done, and rooms decorated.

Exercise

What do you rate as the advantages and disadvantages of living at home at the moment? If you could afford it, would you prefer to rent a bed-sit? Why, or why not?

Costs

Having a place of your own can be an expensive business. Here are some of the costs that you might face:

a Rent or mortgage repayments. This may be paid weekly but more likely it will be monthly. If you are young and looking around for accommodation, the mortgage repayments on a house are likely to be more than the rent for similar accommodation. One of the advantages of buying your own house, of course, is that eventually you will repay the whole of the mortgage, and then you won't have to pay anything.

b Rates. You could pay two types of rates. Water rates pay for the water you use and local authority rates pay for local authority services, like schools, street lighting, roads and libraries. They are calculated on the size of your property—the larger the property, the more rates you will have to pay. You can pay them either monthly or in twice-yearly instalments. If you hire rented accommodation, rates will most likely be paid by your landlord—but check on this when you're thinking of renting somewhere.

c Repairs and maintenance—everything from decorating to mending the roof, fixing the toilet and looking after the garden. If you live in rented accommodation, this should mostly be the responsibility of the landlord **but** it may be easier or quicker to do simple jobs yourself.

d House insurance—dealt with in the next section.

In general, buying a house is much more expensive than renting to start with, but if you buy a house in your mid-twenties, you should find that, twenty years later, buying a house is cheaper than renting. If you buy a house, you're the owner of a valuable piece of property which you could, of course, sell if you want to and spend the money. If you rent, you will never come to own a valuable property. Owning your own home means greater freedom—you can decide what colour to paint your house, whether or not to have pets, whether to extend your house and so on. It is perhaps not surprising that most people would eventually like to buy their own house.

Exercise

Using information from your local paper or local estate agent, describe **five** different houses on sale in your local area at the moment. Why do the prices of those houses differ?

Insurance

What happens if you have a fire at home which destroys your house, or the pipes burst and ruin your furniture? If you've been prudent, you need not suffer any financial loss because you will have insured your house and its contents.

An insurance company is like a big disaster club. Everybody belonging to the club pays in a regular amount of money, called 'premiums'. This money is then used to compensate those members of the club who have suffered disaster, and to pay for the running expenses of the club.

Whether renting or buying a house, it's a good idea to insure the contents of your house—everything from the television to the carpets to the lampshade. In return for your premium, the insurance company will issue you with a policy. This is a legal contract which explains under what circumstances you can make a claim on the insurance company, and on what basis the company will decide how much to give you for what has happened. If you own a house, you will certainly want to insure your house too—against dangers like fire, flood and malicious damage. Hunt around for the cheapest insurance policy because there are quite large differences in premiums between different companies for the same type of insurance. A good place to start would be the latest *Which?* magazine report on household insurance, available from your local public library.

Exercise

Find out what insurance your parents have, and the cost and cover of that insurance.

Obtaining accommodation

You've decided whether to rent or buy, and what sort of accommodation you want: but how do you set about finding a suitable property? If you're thinking of buying somewhere, getting hold of information is quite easy. Local newspapers, estate agents and sale boards outside houses will all give information about houses for sale. If you want rented accommodation, matters are a little more difficult: there is a shortage of good rented accommodation in most parts of Britain. So, you need to keep a keen eye on advertisements in local newspapers and local shops (particularly post offices). Also, keep your ear to the ground: many people find rented accommodation through a friend, or a friend of a friend knowing somewhere which may not even be advertised. If you do see an advertisement for a place you think you might like, don't waste any time. Telephone or go round as soon as you can or you might find the place is already gone.

Finally, if you are unemployed or on social security, the Department of Health and Social Security or your local council may well pay part or all of your rent. Find out what you are entitled to before you make any decisions to rent a property.

Important points to keep in mind

1. There are two basic choices which can be made when obtaining accommodation—either owning your own home or renting.

2. Buying your own home is initially far more expensive but is likely to be cheaper in the long term.

3. Rented accommodation is often difficult to obtain, particularly council accommodation, so be prepared to spend a great deal of time and effort looking for the right accommodation.

4. Insuring your possessions is highly desirable.

35

House-hunting

John Hill aged 19 and single, works as a trainee sales representative for a local firm selling home improvements. He earns on average £70 a week after tax and other deductions. He thinks he may move to another area within a few years. Currently living in rented accommodation.

Jane Last aged 21, single, a nurse. She earns an average take-home pay of £60 a week. She's unlikely to move hospitals in the foreseeable future. She wouldn't like to live on her own. Currently living in accommodation at the hospital.

Paul and Mary Williams married for two years. He's a fitter at a local engineering company earning take-home pay of £100 a week; she's a secretary at the same firm earning £70 a week take-home pay. She'd like to give up work soon to have a baby. They'd really like to buy somewhere of their own but don't know whether they can afford it or not.

Robert and Sarah Hayes married for ten years. He's a refuse collector and she is a housewife. They have two small children aged 6 and 2. They are living in a two-bedroomed rented flat at the moment and would like to move out to something larger. They've got £2000 in savings.

Chris Armstrong and Sue Long aged 22 and 20. They want to start living together. He's a garage mechanic earning £90 a week after tax and deductions and she's a shop assistant earning £60 a week after tax and deductions.

Ray and Helen Gough aged 45 and 42. He's a teacher earning £120 a week after tax and deductions. She's a housewife. They have two children aged 16 and 18 still living at home. They are presently living in a four-bedroomed house of their own worth about £65 000 with a £2000 mortgage still outstanding.

Roger and Andrea Tucker aged 60 and 58. He's unemployed but she's still earning £80 a week. All their children have now left home. Their three-bedroomed detached house would fetch about £40 000.

Bill Harrier aged 68, retired and single, living off his state old-age pension and his savings—earning about £40 a week. Currently living in rented accommodation.

Accommodation

Bradmore 61 Bridge Lane, single fully furnished flat, rent £26 per week, five weeks in advance, working person only.

Nice bedsitter suitable man or two friends, £25 per week—apply Saturday morning 11.00 a.m.

Wolverhampton two-bed house, rates paid, own phone, £45 per week.

Willenhall three-bedroom semi-detached, pets accepted, garage, rates included, only £45 per week.

Dudley luxurious two-bedroom apartment on two levels. Ground floor comprises fully-fitted kitchen, large lounge/dining room and spacious hall with feature spiral staircase. Upper level includes fully-fitted bathroom with coloured suite and two large bedrooms. Must be viewed. Under our special mortgage subsidy scheme, first year's mortgage from only £28.40 per week to suitable applicant. Ask for full details.

Oldbury 69 Chapel Road. Middle terraced house close to local shopping facilities and schools. Comprising lounge with stone fireplace and double-glazed bay window, living room, kitchen, two bedrooms with double glazing, bathroom with suite and shower, rear garden. Mortgage available. Vacant possession. £11 500.

Wolverhampton 14 White St. Fully modernized terraced house with front and rear reception rooms, kitchen, bathroom, three bedrooms and good sized rear garden. £10 500.

Bedsits West Park, Wolverhampton, suit older workmen, all facilities, £18 per week, four weeks in advance.

Wolverhampton 3 Siegfried Drive—attractive modern semi in good condition, full gas central heating, full lounge, dining kitchen, garage, large rear garden £30 000.

Wolverhampton 3 Rogers Close—spacious three-bedroomed bungalow, full gas central heating, lounge, large kitchen, well stocked garden, offers in the region of £40 000.

TASK

State which accommodation would suit the eight people/families, and why. *Note:* you may well decide that two or more types of accommodation may suit one or more of them, or that none is suitable.

Tim and Jennie

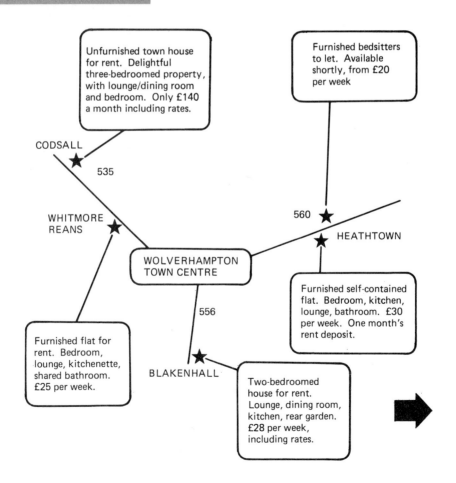

Unfurnished town house for rent. Delightful three-bedroomed property, with lounge/dining room and bedroom. Only £140 a month including rates.

Furnished bedsitters to let. Available shortly, from £20 per week

CODSALL
535

WHITMORE REANS

560

HEATHTOWN

WOLVERHAMPTON TOWN CENTRE

Furnished self-contained flat. Bedroom, kitchen, lounge, bathroom. £30 per week. One month's rent deposit.

556

Furnished flat for rent. Bedroom, lounge, kitchenette, shared bathroom. £25 per week.

BLAKENHALL

Two-bedroomed house for rent. Lounge, dining room, kitchen, rear garden. £28 per week, including rates.

Bus service		Single fare (pence)	Approximate journey time (minutes)
535	Codsall to Wolverhampton	75	30
	Codsall to Whitmore Reans	65	20
	Whitmore Reans to Wolverhampton	22	10
558	Blakenhall to Wolverhampton	22	7
560	Heathtown to Wolverhampton	22	5

TASK

Tim and Jennie are looking for somewhere to live. He earns £70 a week and she earns £50 a week, after tax and deductions. He works in Heathtown and she works in Codsall. Which of the flats or houses do you think they ought to rent? They have no savings and no furniture. Explain your reasons carefully.

Buy or rent?

Calendar monthly payment of principal and interest

NET RATE OF INTEREST 9.975% PER ANNUM

Term					Amount of loan
5 yrs £	10 yrs £	15 yrs £	20 yrs £	25 yrs £	£
2.20	1.36	1.09	0.98	0.92	100
5.49	3.39	2.74	2.44	2.29	250
10.99	6.78	5.47	4.89	4.59	500
21.97	13.55	10.94	9.77	9.17	1 000
54.93	33.88	27.35	24.43	22.93	2 500
109.85	67.75	54.70	48.85	45.85	5 000
219.70	135.50	109.40	97.70	91.70	10 000
329.55	203.25	164.10	146.55	137.55	15 000
439.40	271.00	218.80	218.80	183.40	20 000
549.25	338.75	273.50	244.25	229.25	25 000
659.10	406.50	328.20	293.10	275.10	30 000

Source: Midshires Building Society

Frank Innes

A Black Horse Agency

10 Lichfield Street
Wolverhampton
WV1 1DG
Tel: Wolverhampton (0902) 25222

S.4943
FREEHOLD

VACANT
POSSESSION

39

PRICE: Offers around £9,500
VIEWING: By key to be accompanied.

GENERAL INFORMATION:

A TWO BEDROOMED END TOWN HOUSE conveniently located just off the Cannock Road and being within a short walking distance of local shops, schools and regular bus service to Wolverhampton town centre. The property is constructed of brick beneath a roof of slate and the accommodation briefly comprises FRONT SITTING ROOM with fitted gas fire, REAR LIVING ROOM also with fitted gas fire, KITCHEN with stainless steel sink unit, BATHROOM with complete modern suite. There is a medium sized private rear garden which backs directly onto open playing fields.
DIRECTIONAL NOTES:
The approach from Wolverhampton is via the Wednesfield Road and after approximately half a mile turn left into Woden Road.
SERVICES:
All mains services are connected.
CURRENT RATES INFORMATION:
R.V. £86.00
Half yearly general rates £64.93
Half yearly water charges £14.19

ACCOMMODATION:

Half glazed door to

FRONT SITTING ROOM 12′6″ x 10′ fitted gas fire in polished wood surround with illuminated log effect, picture window.

INNER LOBBY floor to ceiling built in cupboard access to cellar off beneath stairs.

REAR LIVING ROOM 12′8″ x 11′3″ fitted gas fire in polished wood surround enclosed stairs to first floor off.

KITCHEN 8′9″ x 6′1″ having a thermoplastic tiled floor, stainless steel sinkunit (H&C tiled splash back and sill) incorporating under cupboards, adjacent base unit and formica work surface, gas cooker point.

REAR HALL with wall mounted Main Bristol gas water heater, half glazed door to the rear garden.

BATHROOM with panelled bath, pedestal wash basin (H&C and tile surround to each) low suite w.c.

On the First Floor

LANDING

FRONT BEDROOM 1. 14′9″ x 10′.

REAR BEDROOM 2. 14′8″ x 11′3″ built in storage cupboard.

OUTSIDE

There is a medium sized rear garden which backs directly onto playing fields. Rear pedestrian access is provided.

7364

WOLVERHAMPTON, WALSALL, BIRMINGHAM, BURTON-UPON-TRENT, DERBY, NOTTINGHAM, LEICESTER, LOUGHBOROUGH, MELTON MOWBRAY, LONG EATON, BEESTON, BELPER, MANSFIELD, SUTTON-IN-ASHFIELD, CHESTERFIELD.

FOR CONDITIONS PLEASE SEE OVER

Source: Frank Innes

TASK

Look at the house details and the mortgage repayment tables. An identical house could be rented from a private landlord for £25 a week including repairs, rates and water rates. Assume that the house would cost £300 a year on average to maintain. Would it be better to rent or buy (a) now, (b) in 15 years' time, (c) in 30 years' time? Explain your answer carefully.

Insurance renewal

TASK

1. What is the purpose of insurance?
2. What difficulties did this family face?
3. Did they make the wrong decision about their insurance renewal or were they just unlucky?

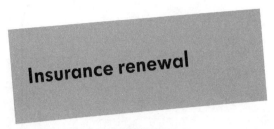

No smoke without fire?

8 Primrose Street
Wolverhampton
Tel: (0902) 684236
19-6-86

Dear Mags,

I've got bad news to tell you. It was Tuesday night: the whole lot went up in flames. I blame it on Bert Reynolds—the thin man who lives next door at number 10. Never have liked smokers and there he was puffing away non-stop. I think he must have let drop his fag end on to the sofa. I mean, there was nobody else smoking in the sitting room. The smell was terrible, and the smoke that came from that sofa—you wouldn't believe it. Lucky that Jim had a fire extinguisher in the kitchen. What gets me is that we'd only just had the room decorated—not cheap either at £150—and the wallpaper was ruined. Not to mention the sofa—brand new it was. Jim's birthday present to me. Had to save up £450 for that. That's a 9th April I won't forget in a hurry. And that's the last time Bert gets invited to one of our parties. Bloody smokers!

Love

Phyllis

TASK

Fill in as much as you can of the Personal Property Claim Form from the details given in the letter. Phyllis Brown is the owner of her own house and her policy number is 756782350. Why does this sort of incident illustrate the importance of having insurance?

Personal property insurance claim

Royal Insurance

Branch Address

Personal Property Claim Form

To assist you in completing this form and preparing your claim please read the notes attached.

SECTION 1 – DETAILS OF POLICYHOLDER & POLICY

Name ....

Address ....

....

.... Postal Code ....

Name of Building Society (if any) ....

Telephone No. where we may contact you between 9.00 a.m. and 5.00 p.m.

STD Code (.............) Tel. No. ....

Policy No.

OR

Mortgage Account No.

SECTION 2 – DETAILS OF WHEN, WHERE & HOW LOSS/DAMAGE HAPPENED

Date of loss/damage

Where did loss/damage happen?

How did the loss/damage happen? (If theft from a building, give details of how entry was gained).

If caused by someone who is not a member of your household, e.g. tradesman, give name and address.

Name ....

Address ....

....

IF PROPERTY WAS LOST OR STOLEN, PLEASE ANSWER THE FOLLOWING QUESTIONS.

Were the police notified? | YES | NO | Delete as appropriate

When and at what Police Station was report made?   Date/Time ..../.............. Police Station ....

If theft from the Insured Address, is the property lent, let, or sublet? | YES | NO | Delete as appropriate

Source: Royal Insurance Company

5 Why work?

Alternatives

Economics is the study of the allocation of scarce resources. Your time and your energies are scarce. If you choose to go out to a disco tonight, you can't spend the night at home watching television. If you choose to go out to work, you can't spend all your time at home in leisure activities. If you choose to have a career in bricklaying, you can't join the police force at the same time. You have to decide how to allocate your time, and that involves choice. And every choice has an opportunity cost—the most desirable alternative which has to be given up because of a decision that you've made.

With regard to work, what are the realistic choices for young people today? These can be grouped into three major categories: going out to work for money, staying at home, or carrying on with education. If you decide to go out to work, you're likely to do so because you want to earn money and because you enjoy your job. Both of these points are discussed later on in this chapter, and in other chapters. So, let's look more closely at the other two alternatives.

Staying at home can mean many different things to different people. For a 16- or 17-year-old, it's likely to mean unemployment, which is undesirable for a large number of reasons. State benefits for being unemployed are so low in today's Britain that unemployment and poverty go hand in hand; certainly supplementary benefit for 16–18-year-olds is very low indeed. Unemployment leads to lack of job experience which in turn makes it more difficult to get the sort of job the person wants. It also leads to personal and psychological difficulties as the unemployed person feels rejected by the society in which he or she lives. It's no coincidence that unemployment is associated with a higher risk of illness and suicide.

Not having a paid job doesn't, of course, mean that you are necessarily unemployed. Less than half the population in Britain has paid jobs. The rest are children under 16, the 16s and over in education, housepersons, retired people, etc. Many of the worst effects of unemployment can be countered if the unemployed person can become a houseperson, retired, etc. What this means is that the unemployed person finds a major role for him or herself which is not going out to work. So, an unemployed 17-year-old may, for instance, run the house for his or her parents—who may both go out to work. Or a 17-year-old may concentrate on leisure activities—walking, reading, gardening, listening to music, motor mechanics, travelling; or an unemployed person could fill his or her time by undertaking unpaid voluntary work. All of these options mean that the unemployed person has a serious interest in life. The worst problems of unemployment occur when the unemployed feel that life has nothing to offer them, and that life is meaningless.

Exercise

If you became unemployed when you were 16 or 18, what would you do with your time? Would you regard the experience as a waste of time, a fill-in while you were waiting to get a job or a positive experience?

Carrying on with education

This has two advantages. Firstly, education is enjoyable in its own right. Having experienced it for over 11 years, you might find this difficult to believe and your sights might be set only on the day when you can leave school or college. But, millions of adults in Britain have at some time or other attended evening classes and paid for the privilege! Many of your contemporaries will be trying to get into polytechnic or university for yet another three years or more of education. And you yourselves will have found some parts of your education interesting and stimulating.

Exercise

How long do you wish to stay on in education? What do you see as the advantages and disadvantages of staying on for yourself?

Job satisfaction

Leisure and education are all very well but the vast majority of young people will want to have a job of some sort eventually. Why is this? Most people go out to work, not only because they are paid for it, but also because they enjoy part or all of their work. 'Job satisfaction' is the term used to describe this enjoyment of the job. A large number of different factors contribute to job satisfaction, including:

◆ The responsibilities of the job. The important factor here is how much control you have over how you organize and do your job. If you have responsibility for your job, you will gain more job satisfaction than if everything is decided for you.

◆ Contact with people. Some people like to have contact with others in their job, others don't. Getting the right amount helps contribute towards job satisfaction.

◆ The variety of tasks in a job. If you are performing the same task day in day out, hour by hour, minute by minute, then the job rapidly becomes boring. One of the problems with assembly-line work is that most work is routine and repetitious. Imagine making television sets where your job is to perform one simple task, which takes 30 seconds. Assuming an 8-hour day, 5-day week, 46-week year, you'll be performing the same simple task 960 times a day, or 4800 times a week, or 220 800 times a year—which all adds up to a very boring job!

◆ Pay, promotion prospects, working hours, holidays, conditions of service—the higher the pay, the better the promotion prospects, etc. the more job satisfaction you are likely to get.

◆ Job security—in these days of high unemployment, job security is an important contributing factor to job satisfaction.

Pay

One reason, if not the main one, for people going out to work is to earn money. There are many technical terms associated with pay. Here are those you are most likely to come across when you go out to work.

◆ Basic pay—pay received for working the standard working period, say 40 hours a week.

◆ Overtime pay—pay received for working overtime. Often this is paid at a higher rate than the standard wage rate.

◆ Wage rate—the amount of money received for working a fixed period of time. Wage rates are usually expressed in terms of so many pounds per hour.

◆ Bonus payments or allowances—payments over and above basic pay. These could arise from a variety of sources including productivity agreements (relating bonus payments to the amount produced by a worker or group of workers), payments for working unsocial hours (such as night shifts) and commission (payment for selling so many items).

◆ Piece rates—a worker is paid by the number of items produced, rather than by the number of hours worked.

◆ Deductions—money taken away from your pay. Three major deductions are income tax (payable at 29% on part of your income), national insurance contributions (to pay for benefits such as unemployment benefit and the state retirement pension) and superannuation payments (payments into a pension fund).

◆ Gross earnings—basic pay plus additional payments like overtime before deductions have been taken away.

◆ Net earnings or take-home pay—gross pay after deductions such as income tax.

- ◆ Salaries—a salary tends to be paid to a white-collar worker, such as a teacher, a manager or a doctor. It is paid monthly unlike a wage which is usually paid weekly.

- ◆ Fringe benefits—these are non-monetary payments, like a company car, or luncheon vouchers or a free pension scheme. Fringe benefits such as a company car can be worth thousands of pounds a year to a worker.

When choosing a job it is important to find out what exactly are the rates of pay and the conditions of service. If you are interviewed for a job, do not be afraid to ask for details—if nothing else, it will look to the interviewer as though you are interested in the job!

Self-employment

The vast majority of workers in this country—23 million in 1986—are classed as employees: that is, they work for somebody else, their employers. The other 2 million are classed as self-employed—they work for themselves. Will you become an employee or choose self-employment when you start work?

There are a number of advantages to being self-employed. One major advantage for most self-employed workers is that they are their own boss. They can choose when to work or how hard to work; if they feel like a longer lunch break or want to 'knock off' early, they don't have to ask any boss—they have the freedom to choose for themselves. Another advantage is that if the business goes well the self-employed person will reap the benefits.

But self-employment also poses a number of problems. While being your own boss means greater freedom and choice, it also carries responsibilities. You will have to take responsibility for organizing your business. You may well find that you work much harder being your own boss than if you worked for somebody else. And it's all very well thinking of the times when your business is prospering, but you also have to take into account the fact that your business may do badly or even fail. If your business fails, you could end up being declared bankrupt and lose all your possessions.

You will also face other financial problems that an employee would not face. You may have to find a considerable amount of money to start up your business. You will also need to think carefully about your long-term future. What will happen when you retire? What happens if you have a serious illness and can't run your business for a long time? You will need to set aside money for these eventualities—but that, of course, reduces your take-home earnings.

If you do want to become self-employed, what's the best way to go about it? You're going to have a head start if you're already familiar with the world of self-employment. Many self-employed people today grew into their job by starting off working for their father or other member of the family who themselves were self-employed. Or you might work in a small firm where you can become familiar with all the responsibilities and possibilities of self-employment. If you don't have these advantages, you could try and talk with people who are self-employed—a member of the family perhaps, or a neighbour or a local small shopkeeper. You also need to decide upon what you are going to do as a self-employed person. Your choice will obviously be affected by your talents, qualifications and experience. It's no good setting yourself up as an electrician if you don't know how to wire a plug! Because experience is so important, many people who become self-employed only do so once they've already worked for somebody else for a fair length of time. There are some jobs where experience counts for little—window cleaning or simple gardening are two examples—but most self-employed people are skilled, not unskilled, workers.

Once you've decided what you might do, you should then investigate whether or not a market exists for what you wish to produce or sell. You might be an electrician working for a small local firm. Is there enough work for both your existing employer and you in the locality? If you set up elsewhere, is there enough work for you there? You must be totally realistic about the size of your market—a failure here at the planning stage could result in a quick end to your hopes.

Then you need to sort out all the practical details of setting yourself up. Have you got the money to buy necessary equipment and stock and keep your business running while in its infancy? Have you filled in all the government forms necessary to set up a small business? Have you got all the necessary permissions from planning authorities? Have you bought necessary equipment and stock and made efforts to secure orders for when you start?

Becoming self-employed is no easy task and risk is a fact of life for the self-employed. Careful planning is essential if your business is to be a success.

Exercise

Would you consider becoming self-employed? If yes, what would you consider doing and why? If not, why not?

Important points to keep in mind

1. At 16, you have a choice about what to do with your time—will you stay on at school, become unemployed or start work?

2. Not having a job can be a positive experience if you choose to make it positive.

3. Education will help you to develop not only intellectually but also as a whole person.

4. Getting a job will give you pay and hopefully also some job satisfaction.
   You may decide to become self-employed, but the easiest route to this is via working for somebody else.

The penalties of motherhood

By Robin Pauley

In an analysis of women in paid employment for the Centre for Economic Policy Research, Heather Joshi estimates that mothers with average earnings potential lose £50,000 in lifetime earnings by raising two children, rising to £62,000 for three children as the table shows.

The most recent edition of Social Trends shows that about 50 per cent of all married mothers work full or part time. Most work full time until the birth of the first child, and around 90 per cent return to work afterwards, a proportion which has not changed much since the 1940s.

However, Heather Joshi's research shows just what the cost of this interrupted work pattern is for the women and families involved. Employed mothers often work part-time while childless women seldom

do. Workers who follow an uninterrupted career pattern often achieve higher pay rates through promotion, seniority or experience, opportunities which are foregone by women who opt for a period of childraising. Women returning to work often accept poorly paid, part-time jobs which do not fully utilise their skills or training in order to fit employment into the family roles.

A statistical analysis of a hypothetical adult life pattern by Ms Joshi shows a mother of two spending six fewer years at work than her childless counterpart—close to the statistical findings in Social Trends. This results from the loss of nine years of full-time work offset by a gain of three years of part time. The average hourly pay after age 25 was reduced by 6 per cent, 8 per cent and 11 per cent for mothers of one, two and three children respectively compared with childless counterparts.

Opportunity costs of bearing and rearing children compared to remaining childless over ages 25 to 59

	1	2	2	3	3
Number of births	1	2	2	3	3
Years between births		2	3	2	3
Years of employment foregone (full-time equivalent)	5.3	6.9	7.4	7.9	9.5
Earned income foregone compared with childless counterpart, £000*	35	46	49	52	62

*1985 prices assuming £5,000 a year as full-time salary at age 24.
(*The Financial Times*, 31 January 1985)

TASK

1 What percentage of married mothers:

    a work full or part-time;
    b work after they have had children?

2 Give **four** reasons why women who return to work after having children earn less on average than women who don't leave work for a time to bring up children.

3 How many fewer years did a mother of two work in paid employment than childless women in work, according to Ms Joshi?

4 *a* What was the average percentage reduction in the hourly rate of pay experienced by a mother with two children?

    b If the average weekly rate of pay for a career woman over 25 was £100, how much on average was the rate of pay for a woman who had two children?

5 *a* What is meant by 'opportunity cost'?
    b What, according to the table, is the opportunity cost for a woman of having 1 child, or 3 children assuming a 3-year interval between each child?

6 What would happen to the opportunity cost of having children if:

    a prices remained at 1985 levels but a female full-time salary at age 24 rose from £5000 to £7500?

    b a woman had 3 children spaced at 5-year intervals and she didn't work during the period?

7 Given the high cost of taking time off to look after children, why do women choose to do this?

Job Hunting

Source: Daily Mail, 24 April 1985

PRODUCTION FOREMAN

Salary £7,600 per annum

Required for the assembly of special purpose blasting machines.
An experienced
FOREMAN (male/female)
With knowledge of fitting, welding and fabrication in a jobbing environment.

Applications including brief career details to:

**D. J. Smith, Personnel Manager,
ABRASIVE DEVELOPMENTS LTD.,
Norman House, Henley-in-Arden,
Solihull, West Midlands B95 5AH.**

Previous applicants for this position should not re-apply.

Source: The Birmingham Post, 15 December 1984

NATIONAL ASSOCIATION OF TEACHERS IN FURTHER AND HIGHER EDUCATION

requires at its Headquarters in Euston/Kings Cross

a SECRETARY

Applicants should be competent audio-typists with a good telephone manner and appropriate secretarial experience (preferably including an understanding of committee work). They should have already achieved a high degree of organisational efficiency.

Good conditions, own office, $32\frac{1}{2}$ hour work, LVs, 20 days leave. Salary not less than £7,170 pa gross.

Please write for application form to **Room 316, NATFHE, Hamilton House, Mabledon Place, London WC2H 9BH.** Closing date for completed applications is 30 April 1985.

NATFHE is an equal opportunities employer.

Source: The Guardian, 22 April 1985

REPORTER

Radio Newcastle

Have you got what it takes to work on Wearside? If so, Radio Newcastle, the voice of the North East, is looking for a reporter to work out of their busy Sunderland studio. The work is primarily reporting, interviewing and bulletin writing. At least three years' journalistic experience, good microphone voice and current driving licence essential.

Salary £8,038–£9,552 (currently under review) plus allowance of £537 p.a. Relocation expenses considered.

Contact us immediately for application form (quote ref. 2386/G and enclose s.a.e.): **BBC Appointments, London W1A 1AA.** Tel. 01-927 5799.

We are an equal opportunities employer

TASK

Read the advertisements carefully:

◆ Compare the pay and conditions for the jobs described.
◆ Which job do you think provides the highest total benefits for the work involved?

50

NAME
_____

EMPLOYEE NUMBER
_____

TAX CODE
_____

N.I. NUMBER
_____

PAY DATE
_____

CREDITS	AMOUNT	DEBITS	AMOUNT
Basic		Tax	
Overtime		N.I.	
Bonus		Pension	
		Union Dues	
Total		Total	

NET PAY
_____

Helen Adams
Ms Helen Adams works for Huberts' plc, a large engineering
company, as an electrician. She is paid every Thursday, this Thursday
being 25 July 1985. Her basic wage is £120 a week for a 40-hour
week. Last week she worked 4 hours' overtime paid at time and a
half. As an electrician, she is entitled to participate in the company
pension scheme which costs her 5% of her gross earnings. Her
national insurance number is CZ 82 41 82 A, her work number 006274,
and her union membership number (she pays 50p a week in union
dues) is HA 2001. Her tax allowances for the year are £3120.

Peter Watkins

Mr Watkins is a shop assistant working for J. Spooners', a regional chain of supermarkets. His duties include stacking shelves, working the till and dealing with deliveries. Every morning he has to 'clock on' and his clocking-on card gives his name, his works number (01828) and the times of arrival and departure from work. His card last week showed that he worked 48 hours. His basic working week is only 38 hours. Pay day is every Friday. Peter Watkins' union, to which he subscribes 70p a week through his pay packet, is currently negotiating a pay rise. It wants to increase wage rates from the current £3 an hour to £3.50 an hour and increase overtime pay from time and a quarter to time and a half. Peter is able to earn £50 a week tax-free. His firm doesn't provide any company pension, so he pays into the state earnings-related scheme. His national insurance number is AB 40 60 80 BZ. Pay day is this coming Friday.

51

TASK

Copy out the Work Pay Slip reproduced above and then fill in the details for each of the workers. Read carefully the information on income tax and national insurance contributions before calculating the debits on the pay slip.

Notes

Income tax

Income tax, as the name implies, is a tax on a person's income. The standard rate of tax (at March 1986) is 29%. So for every £1 that a worker earns, 29p goes to the Inland Revenue (the tax collection department of the government) and 71p is kept by the worker. The worker, however, does **not** have to pay 29% on all his income. He or she is allowed to earn a certain amount tax-free—this sum of money is called an **allowance**. For instance, if a worker's tax allowance were £3000 a year and he or she earned £13 000, then only £10 000 would be taxable and the tax payable would be 29% of £10 000, or £3000. Income tax allowances are shown on the pay slip by the **tax code**. This is the yearly value of the tax allowance with the last digit deleted. So £3000 worth of tax allowances would be shown as a tax code of 300, £3555 worth of tax allowances would be shown as a tax code of 355.

National insurance contributions

All employees who earn more than £38.00 (in 1986) a week have to pay national insurance contributions which go to pay for benefits such as unemployment benefit and the basic state retirement pension. Employees who form part of a company pension scheme pay reduced-rate national insurance contributions—6.85% of gross earnings. Employees who are not part of a company pension scheme have to contribute to the state earnings-related pension scheme and are charged up to 9% of their gross earnings.

Interview of self-employed person

The aim is to help you familiarize yourself with the world of self-employment. This will be done by interviewing a self-employed person.

TASK 1

Construct a questionnaire for your interview. Firstly, make a rough draft of the questions you will put to your interviewee. These questions are likely to revolve around the following points:

earnings, hours of work, numbers of employees, job satisfaction, tax position, VAT, national insurance contributions, income tax, nature of work undertaken, starting up capital, investment, bank, prices, turnover, costs, profit, wages, business premises, customers, advertising and promotion, area of work, competition, bankruptcy, accountants, production processes, work routines.

Decide in what order you will ask your questions, check your English, make sure there is no overlap between your questions and write them out neatly in their proper order. Allow a space between each question in which to put the answer.

TASK 2

Decide whom you will interview. This could be a friend of the family, somebody you work for, the owner of a local shop where you make purchases, or a friend of a friend. He or she must of course be self-employed! Then make an approach to the person. Ask as politely as possible. Arrange a date, and a place to conduct the interview.

TASK 3

Conduct the interview. Explain why you are conducting it and that you will be making a record of answers given. Put your questions as politely as possible. Expect your interviewee to reply to some questions by saying that the information is confidential and not to be divulged. Don't be afraid to ask supplementary questions and to repeat a question if the interviewee fails to answer directly. Record all the answers on your question sheet. You may prefer to tape-record the interview, but do ask permission first. At the end, thank the interviewee for giving up his or her time to help you.

TASK 4

Write a 1000-word report about the work of the self-employed person you have interviewed.

Your own business

This will help you to draw up a plan for launching a business of your own and provide a means of checking the success or failure of that business.

TASK 1

Answer the following questions:

1. Make a list of the qualifications you hope to have when you first start working. What qualifications, if any, do you hope to get while you are employed?

2. What job experience have you already had?

3. What aspects of a particular occupation would give you job satisfaction?

4. What do you consider to be your main strengths as a person? What are your main weaknesses? (Words you might consider using are 'physically strong', 'indecisive', 'self-willed', 'sociable', 'good planner', 'nervous', 'methodical', 'not very bright'.

5. What skills do you possess? (You might find it helpful here to list these under three main headings: academic skills, such as being good at maths or good at communicating; manual skills, such as being good at woodwork or at mending electronic equipment; and social skills, such as making people feel happy when they are with you, or motivating others to complete a task.)

6. What jobs would you be interested in doing when you leave education?

TASK 2

Decide upon **one** self-employed job you would like to have. Find out:

- What qualifications, if any, you have to have for the job;

- What previous job experience it is desirable or necessary to have had;

- What gives it job satisfaction;

- What personal characteristics are important to the job;

- What skills are necessary;

- What similar jobs could you do as an employed person.

Then compare your answers to Task 1 with your answers here. Would you be the right person for this job?

54

TASK 3

Find out what it would take to set yourself up as a self-employed person in your chosen occupation. Consider:

◆ What would be the financial cost of starting up?

◆ Where would you get the money from to start up on your own?

◆ What professional requirements, if any, would have to be satisfied?

◆ Would you have to go into partnership with other people or would you have to employ other workers?

◆ What competition could you expect from other businesses?

◆ Where would you locate your business and over what area would it sell products?

◆ What advertising and other forms of promotion would be necessary?

◆ What sources of outside help could you call upon to start up and to run the business?

◆ What running costs would the business face? Include your own salary.

◆ How would you decide what price to set for your products?

TASK 4

How would you decide whether or not your business was successful? You might consider:

◆ profit and loss accounts

◆ growth of business

◆ hours worked by yourself

◆ the opportunity cost (the next best alternative use) of your time (e.g. another job) and the money tied up in the firm (e.g. the interest to be gained by putting that money in a building society).

6 Where to work

Primary, secondary and tertiary industry

400 years ago in Britain, the single largest employer was the agricultural industry. Agriculture is a part of what is called 'primary industry', an industry which extracts raw materials from the earth. Other examples of primary industry are fishing, mining and oil extractions.

Starting with the Industrial Revolution in the second half of the eighteenth century, more and more jobs were created in the 'secondary' or 'manufacturing' sector of the economy. Workers moved from the countryside into towns to work in the new factories springing up in Britain. In secondary industry, raw materials are transformed into manufactured goods, such as cars, computers, paper and processed food.

Today, British secondary industry is in decline. Two million jobs alone disappeared in manufacturing industry between 1979 and 1984. The largest employer now and for the foreseeable future is 'tertiary' or 'service' industry. This covers a wide range of industries from education and health to retailing (shops) and hairdressing to banking and catering.

There are two main reasons why primary and secondary industry have declined in importance in relative terms. Firstly, it has been much easier to automate (i.e. replace the work that men do by machines) primary and secondary industry than tertiary industry. More and more primary and secondary tasks are being performed by machines. Robotic machines are just the latest development in this long historical process. But, it is much more difficult if not impossible to automate many service sector jobs. The robot teacher, nurse or waiter is still the material of science fiction stories. What's more, it could be that these jobs will never be automated because consumers will want personal service, not robotic service.

The second main reason for the growing relative importance of tertiary industry today is that as consumers have more and more money to spend, they tend to spend much of the increase in their income on services. Rather than demanding more and more cookers, refrigerators or newspapers, consumers want a better health service, or more financial services or more holidays. Because demand for services is growing faster than demand for primary and secondary products, jobs will be created at a faster

TWO ROBOTS APPLY 76 SPOTS OF ADHESIVE TO THE
BONNET OF THE ROVER 200 SERIES AT LONGBRIDGE.

Source: Austin Rover PLC, British Leyl

rate in the tertiary sector of the economy than in the primary and secondary sectors.

Exercise

Make a list of 20 different employers in your locality. Which sectors of industry do these employers belong to?

Small- and large-scale industry

When you do finally manage to get a job, how big will be the size of the place where you work and how big will be your company or employer? The vast majority of work places—factory, office or mine—are relatively small. In 1980, for instance, over half of all factories in British manufacturing industry had less than 10 workers; nine out of every ten factories had less than 100 workers. But these small factories are relatively unimportant both in terms of the numbers of people working there and of their total output. Three-quarters of all workers in manufacturing industry work in the one in ten factories with over 100 workers. Three in ten workers work in factories with over 2000 workers. And these larger factories with over 100 workers produce about 80% of the value of total manufacturing output.

So, the vast majority of work places and firms are relatively small but, equally, they employ relatively few people. Most workers work in the far smaller number of large work places and for companies which are relatively large. The chances are that when you get a job, you will be working for a large employer.

Exercise

Are there any large factories or other work places in your locality employing over 1000 people. If yes, name them and briefly describe the work carried out.

Public services, nationalized enterprises, private firms and co-operatives

The largest single employer in the UK is 'the public sector', a term used to describe the area of the economy managed and owned by government and its agents. This can be broken down into three main parts: central governments, run by politicians at Westminster; local government, run by politicians in town halls up and down the country; and a wide range of individual enterprises such as the BBC, the British Coal Board and the various water boards. The public sector currently spends about £4 in every £10 available for spending on goods and services in the UK.

Jobs with central government include civil service jobs, jobs in the National Health Service and the Armed Forces. Local authorities employ everybody from teachers to refuse collectors to social workers. Nationalized enterprises are companies owned by the government. They include the Central Electricity Generating Board, the National Coal Board, British Steel, the Post Office and British Rail.

Private enterprises or private firms, on the other hand, are firms owned by private individuals and not the state. Household names like ICI, Marks and Spencer, Tube Investments, National Westminster Bank and Cadbury-Schweppes form some of the largest private companies in Britain. These large companies are owned by shareholders who appoint directors to run them. In much smaller private companies, like a small doctors' partnership or a local shop, the owners and the people who run the company are one and the same.

Some workers work for co-operatives. The largest co-operatives in Britain are the retail co-operatives—the chain of shops known as the 'Co-op'. These are owned by the people who shop there, who receive a share of the profits when they buy goods and services. This share is known as the 'dividend' and co-operative societies pay much of this in the form of dividend stamps. A very small number of workers work in owner or worker co-operatives, companies owned by the workers themselves and run by them.

Exercise

List 20 public sector workplaces in your locality and 20 private company works. Are there any co-operatives near you?

Job characteristics

Jobs in different sectors of industry and in different sized firms have different job characteristics. A 'job characteristic' is a particular feature of a job. These different features include whether or not the job

◆ is mainly an outdoor or an indoor job

◆ involves a variety of different tasks or just one or two

◆ involves mainly working with other people or mainly on your own

◆ requires great skill or few skills

◆ requires a long or short training

◆ demands many or few qualifications

◆ is high or low paid

◆ pays regular wages or salaries or pays uneven amounts

◆ has a clear career structure or has few opportunities for promotion

◆ requires workers to pay for materials for their work or all materials are provided by their company

◆ is a job for an employee or for a self-employed person

◆ carries responsibility or not

◆ involves travelling or not

◆ involves regular or irregular hours of work

◆ is likely to lead to membership of a trade union or not

◆ is a full-time or part-time job

◆ is a secure job or not

Exercise

Give the job characteristics of *a* a teacher, *b* a supermarket cashier, and *c* a bricklayer.

Important points to keep in mind

1 **A worker may work in one of the three sectors of industry: primary or extractive industry, secondary or manufacturing industry, and tertiary or service industry.**

2 **Tertiary industry is not only the single largest employer today in Britain, but it is also the sector where the largest growth in new jobs is likely to take place in the future.**

3. Most work places and firms in Britain employ less than 10 workers each but most workers work in work places with over 100 workers.

4. A worker may be employed by central government, local government, a nationalized enterprise or other government body, a private firm or a co-operative.

5. Each job possesses particular job characteristics.

Types of jobs

TASK

1. Describe how employment patterns between primary, secondary and tertiary industry have changed over the period 1955 to 1984.

2. How many people were unemployed in 1985 according to the article?

3. If there were 23 million people in work in 1984, calculate the numbers employed in:

    - agriculture, forestry and fishing
    - manufacturing
    - service

    How many people were self-employed in 1984?

4. Which regions of Britain have been 'most dependent on the older industries' do you think?

5. In 1955 there were 239 000 people unemployed. In 1984, this had risen to 3.2 million. On past evidence, do you think that the growth of self-employment could have a major impact on the unemployment situation?

Source: Department of Employment, *Employment News*, No. 129, March 1985

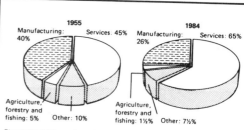

Figures for 1955 on estimated standard industrial classification 1980.

Types of jobs

OF the 26½ million people in the labour force, over 23 million are in work. This is not very different from the total in work 30 years ago; but the similarity masks big changes in the nature and location of jobs.

In 1955 manufacturing accounted for 40 per cent of employees in employment; in 1984, 26 per cent. But the service sector has grown from 45 to 65 per cent.

The sectoral shift has been matched by an occupational shift: even within manufacturing industry a much higher proportion of people are in non-manual occupations, particularly scientific, technological and professional ones.

The number of self-employed has grown markedly too — from 1.7 million in the 1950s to 2.4 million now.

With the change in the industrial balance, there has been a change in the geographical balance, hitting hard those regions most dependent on the older industries. But other regions meanwhile have profited from the growth of new services and high-technology manufacturing.

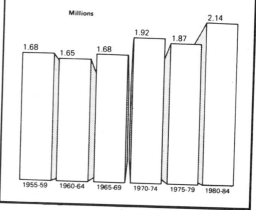

How jobs have shrunk in manufacturing

Source: Department of Employment, *Employment Gazette*, April 1985.

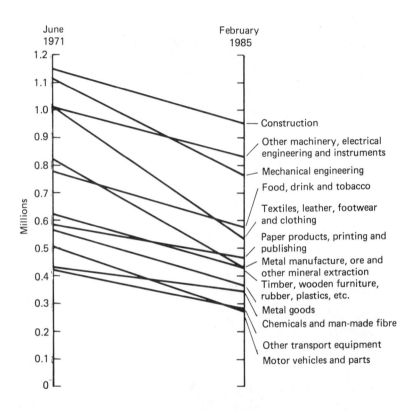

June 1971 / February 1985

Millions

Construction
Other machinery, electrical engineering and instruments
Mechanical engineering
Food, drink and tobacco
Textiles, leather, footwear and clothing
Paper products, printing and publishing
Metal manufacture, ore and other mineral extraction
Timber, wooden furniture, rubber, plastics, etc.
Metal goods
Chemicals and man-made fibre
Other transport equipment
Motor vehicles and parts

TASK

1. Which group of industries employed most workers in (a) 1971 and (b) 1985?

2. Which group of industries employed fewest workers in (a) 1971 and (b) 1985?

3. Which group of industries lost (a) the largest and (b) the smallest number of workers between 1971 and 1985?

4. Calculate the percentage decline in employment in (a) mechanical engineering, (b) motor vehicles and parts, and (c) textiles, leather, footwear and clothing.

5. Roughly how many jobs in total were lost in these industries over the period 1971 to 1985?

6. Give three reasons why the changes shown on the graph are of importance to the UK.

How the service industries have expanded

Source: Department of Employment, *Employment Gazette*, April 1985

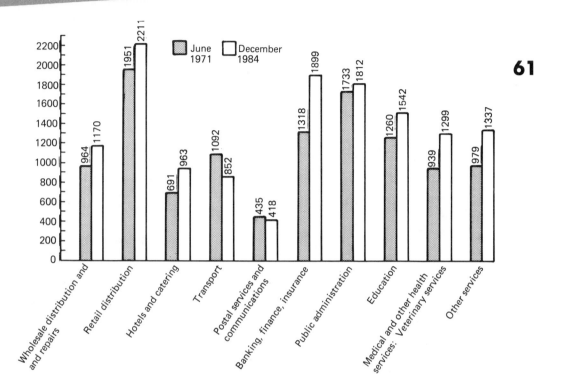

TASK

1. Which was the largest service industry employer in 1984?

2. How many workers were employed in (a) transport in 1971; (b) education in 1984; (c) other services in 1984

3. Which industry saw the largest increase in total number of jobs between 1971 and 1984?

4. Which two service industries saw a small decline in employment?

5. Calculate the percentage increase in employment between 1971 and 1984 in (a) retail distribution; (b) hotels and catering and (c) banking, finance and insurance.

6. Roughly how many jobs were created in service industries over the period 1971 to 1984?

7. Service industries have been called the 'industries of the future'. Which industries do you think will provide new jobs in the future and why?

How to be fruitful and multiply

Martyn Halsall visits a Christian co-operative where a packer earns more than the manager

NEW Testament economics are enjoying a revival in a spice-scented warehouse just off the M1. The Daily Bread Co-operative is a small workers' co-operative, now employing 15 in a former hospital laundry in Northampton. Opened in October, 1980, the Government helped renovate the old laundry, through an MSC project. Half the premises is used as a workshop for people recovering from mental illness and four of them joined Daily Bread for up to six months at a time as part of their rehabilitation.

When it started the co-operative had just three workers, initial sales of £8,000 and a net pre-tax profit of £26. Last year sales were £303,000 and pre-tax profits £10,303. Daily Bread passed its break-even turnover of £250,000 according to plan and now stocks about 150 lines in its cash and carry warehouse. Immediate problems are ethical and logistical rather than commercial. They include the co-operative's future.

It is not just Scriptural tradition but practical psychology which limits the ideal number of people working closely together to around 12. Further growth at Daily Bread might suggest a new co-operative, but one that has an identity of its own and not a satellite, said Mr Sawtell.

Proposals will unfold gradually, at the weekly meeting where all members have an equal voice and vote. Wages are paid on the basis of need rather than occupation.

The basic wage is £86 a week but Mr Sawtell, although the manager, receives only £80 as he has a working wife. Another member, who supports a wife and two children, earns £96 as a packer. The wages policy was decided collectively from Acts: *'and they sold their possessions and goods and distributed them to all, as any had need.'*

The temporary workers on the rehabilitation programme are paid the standard wage and the co-operative also supports Third World development projects, expecting to donate some £3,000 this year — four per cent of the total salary bill. In spite of their low level of salaries by contemporary standards, some co-operative members would like this contribution increased to 10 per cent: the Biblical tithe.

So far they have avoided fork-lift trucks and computers to ensure a simple, labour-intensive style of working. The muesli is mixed by hand, the spices packed without machines and in the spirit of Christian conservation customers are offered refunds on their jars and bottles.

The future seems inevitably to have been spelled out in the first chapter of the Bible: *'and God blessed them saying, Be fruitful and multiply.'*

Source: The Guardian, 24 May 1985

TASK

1. Describe the nature of the business activity of the Daily Bread Co-operative.

2. Imagine you were a worker at the Co-operative. How do you think working there would differ from working for an ordinary company?

3. Explain whether or not you think you would prefer to work in a workers' co-operative rather than for an ordinary firm.

Your ideal job

TASK

1. Write down the job characteristics which you would like your ideal job to possess.

2. Compare the job characteristics of:

   - a secretary/receptionist working for a firm of solicitors
   - a private in the army
   - a teacher in a state primary school
   - a packer on an assembly line producing chocolates

   with your ideal job.

7 At work

In the last chapter various types of business organization were described. All of these organizations have many different aims and objectives, but one which is common to all is 'efficiency'. An organization strives to make the best use of the scarce resources at its disposal. This involves producing the goods and services that its clients (often consumers) want, at the least cost and in the right quantities. In order to allocate scarce resources in the most efficient way, a business needs clear organizational structures. Without these, it will be badly organized and waste scarce resources which could have been used to produce more, cheaper, or better quality goods and services.

Organizational structures

When you first start a job, what organizational structure will you find? How will you fit in? In the first place, the job you do will involve you completing certain tasks. As a shop assistant, you might be responsible for advising customers, selling to customers, and handling receipts as well as cleaning and moving stock. As a secretary, you might be responsible for typing letters and other material, filing and handling incoming phone calls. Your employers will hold you responsible for completing those tasks to a satisfactory standard.

Secondly, there will be workers who are in a position of authority over you, and they have the right to tell you what jobs to do. One day, you might gain promotion and then have people working for you too. Your immediate boss is likely to have a superior over him or her and so it goes on right to the top of the organization.

Exercise

Describe your responsibilities at school or college. Who is in a position of authority over you?

Different chains of command

There are a number of different ways in which this chain of command from the top to the bottom of an organization can be structured. One way is known as 'line' or 'military' organization. The illustration on page 69 shows a pattern of organization for a small company in the garage trade, with several garages selling petrol and cars and repairing and servicing cars. This pattern is a vertical one in which each employee of the company is solely responsible to one person above him or her. This is true from the bottom of the organization right through to the managing director. So, if you were on the till selling petrol, you would be responsible to the sales manager; whereas if you were a mechanic, you would be responsible to the chief mechanic.

This pattern of organization is clear and simple with workers easily able to understand their roles and responsibilities in the firm. A decision once made can be easily communicated to all staff. Work, once delegated, is relatively easy to monitor and control.

Another pattern of organization is called 'functional' organization. **65** In business there are distinct functions: for instance, in a manufacturing company, there might be production, selling and marketing, personnel, accounts, and research and development. In a functional organization, workers have responsibilities for a particular function of the firm. So, an accountant is responsible for accounts, a personnel manager for staff, a production line manager for production and so on. This means that there is no clear line of command in the firm. For instance, workers on a production line might receive orders from the production manager and the personnel officer, as well as the head of research and development. On the other hand, workers have been appointed for their expertise in doing a particular job and this should result in higher efficiency than a pure line organization where a manager may be supervising work about which he or she knows very little.

Most large companies have a mixture of these two types of organization. In line and staff organization, there is a clear chain of command from top to bottom of the company but specialists (the 'staff') have an important advisory role to play. Staff may also have direct control over certain clearly specified areas of line management.

What might all this have to do with you as a new worker in your first job? Assume that you have applied to a large company for a job as a sales person. To start with, there would be a three-year training period with a mixture of on-the-job training and day-release at the local college. The successful applicant would be trained to deal with a wide range of tasks in the sales department, including direct contact with customers, planning sales campaigns, preparation of sales literature and quotations. After this three-year period, the successful applicant would specialize in a particular area of sales work in the company.

Different people will be responsible for interviewing a worker for this post depending upon how the company is organized. In a company which is organized on a line basis, it will be somebody further up the chain of command, such as the sales manager, who will be responsible for this post. In a company organized on a functional basis, it would be the personnel manager who would interview and appoint. But in a typical company organized on a line and staff basis, both the sales manager and the line manager would have responsibilities for appointment.

Exercise

Have you had any interviews for a job? If yes, who interviewed you and what was his/her/their position in the firm or organization? Why were they interviewing you rather than anybody else in the firm?

66

Your boss

If you were appointed, again the type of organization would determine who you would be responsible to. In a line organization, your boss would be the sales manager or one of his assistants; the sales department would be responsible for organizing your training and giving you suitable work experience. In a functional organization, your boss would be the person responsible for training in the company: this might be the personnel manager or it might be a training officer. In a line and staff organization, you might have two bosses, the sales manager and the training officer. The sales manager would be responsible for your work in the office, the training officer for the training aspect of your activities.

How you fitted into the company organization after the three years' training was complete would again depend upon how the company was organized. In a line organized company, you would be solely responsible to your superiors in the sales department; but in staff and line organization, you might also be responsible for some of the jobs you did to workers outside the department, such as the production line manager or the chief accountant.

Discipline at work

One of the major differences between the world of school or college and the world of work is discipline. Many school-leavers find it difficult to adjust to a job because:

◆ hours are long—usually 8 hours a day instead of a typical 5 to 6 hours a day in school

◆ weekend and evening or night work may be required

◆ holidays are only 3 to 4 weeks a year instead of the 14 weeks in education

◆ lateness and absenteeism are offences which can lead to dismissal; in school, it would be extremely difficult to have a pupil expelled for this

◆ workers carry responsibilities: if at school or college, you don't work hard, then the main loser is you yourself; but if you don't work hard in your job, then other workers suffer because they have to fill in and cover for your poor performance; you won't make yourself popular at work with anybody by being lazy and shirking your responsibilities

◆ work is often repetitive and monotonous: if you think sitting in a lesson is boring, think just how boring it would be to sit 8 hours a day performing a simple task like pushing a piece of metal into a machine, pulling a lever and then removing the finished product

Workers can be and are dismissed for a number of reasons. Repeated absence or lateness without good cause is grounds for dismissal. So too is refusal to obey a reasonable instruction. Violence towards other workers or your superiors can lead to instant dismissal. Not doing your job properly could obviously lead to the sack. In most cases, dismissal is not something which occurs without warning. There is usually a series of incidents which build up to a situation where management would consider dismissal. Even then, a three-stage process is often followed. The worker would be given a verbal warning; if the worker belonged to a trade union, then his or her shop steward would normally be present for this warning. If matters did not improve, the worker would be given written warning of dismissal and again the reasons for dismissal would be stated clearly. Only then, assuming that there was no change in the situation, would the worker be dismissed.

67

Exercise

Describe the system of discipline in your school or college. For what can you be disciplined? What are the penalties imposed? Who is responsible for discipline?

Working conditions

Conditions of work vary enormously between different jobs and different employers. To some extent, this is due to the differences in job characteristics discussed in Chapter 6. The conditions of work for a farmworker are very different from those for a university lecturer, for instance. Yet in some ways each worker faces the same questions about conditions of service:

◆ What are the hours of work and the holiday entitlement?

◆ Can any employer order me to work shifts, or work on standby at night or work overtime?

◆ Am I entitled to receive any payment over and above my basic wage or salary?

◆ What are my chances of promotion?

◆ What are my duties and responsibilities in my job?

◆ What procedures exist to assess my performance in the job?

- What disciplinary procedures exist if I fail to do my job properly?

- What period of notice has to be given by me or my employer to terminate the contract of employment?

- Who will represent me in negotiations over pay and other conditions of work?

- What health and safety regulations exist?

As well as all these considerations, the worker is interested in the less formal aspects of working conditions. What are my fellow workers going to be like? How will my superiors treat me? Will the design of the building I work in lead to me being too hot or too cold at work? Will I have to work with anybody who smokes? The amount of satisfaction to be gained from a job will depend not only on the nature of the work but also on these conditions of work.

Exercise Describe the conditions of work at your school or college.

Important points to keep in mind

1. **Organizational structures are needed to make a business efficient.**

2. **These organizational structures tend to be a mixture of line organization and functional organization.**

3. **Work involves discipline. Workers who are undisciplined face the sack.**

4. **Conditions of work form an important part of the job satisfaction to be gained from a job.**

TASK 1

Make a list of the main groups of workers who work solely for your school or college, e.g. teachers/lecturers, cleaning staff.

TASK 2

Make a list of the members of staff of your school or college. Give a brief description of the work of each employee, for example:

Mr Clancy— English teacher
Mr Jones — Caretaker
Mrs Giles —Cook
Mrs Elliott —Secretary

TASK 3

Construct an organizational chart for the school or college. This should show who is responsible to whom and give a brief description of the responsibilities of each worker. This chart need only be a rough sketch. A partially completed example is given opposite.

TASK 4

With your list of names, responsibilities and organizational chart, interview one or more of the workers in your school or college. Check that what you have written down is correct and ask for information which will allow you to complete your organizational chart.

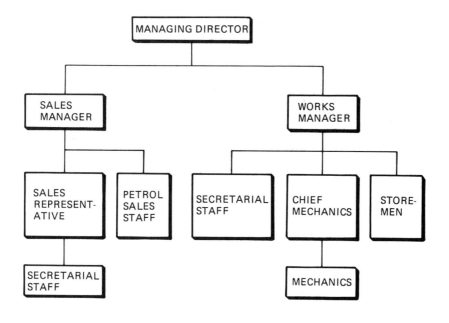

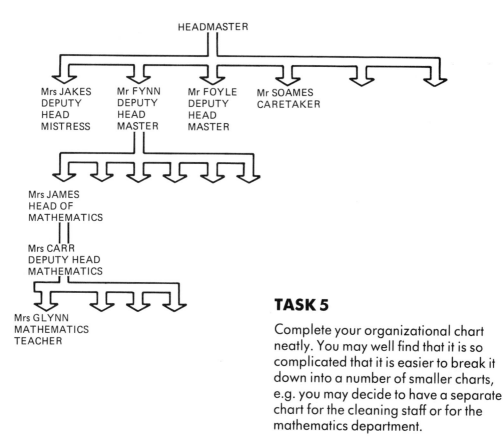

TASK 5

Complete your organizational chart neatly. You may well find that it is so complicated that it is easier to break it down into a number of smaller charts, e.g. you may decide to have a separate chart for the cleaning staff or for the mathematics department.

Interviewing

This project involves interviewing and finding out as much as possible about the duties, demands and responsibilities of a young worker as well as finding out in general about the organizational structure of the work place.

TASK 1

Construct a questionnaire. Questions which you might want to ask could include:

- How did the worker obtain the job? Were there any extra requirements?

- What job does the worker do? What does the job entail?

- Who is the worker answerable to?

- What is the chain of command in the workplace?

- Who does the worker work with?

- What are working conditions like?

- What is the rate of pay? What other benefits can the worker get over and above basic pay?

- What are the training and promotion prospects like?

- What is contained in the contract of work of the employee? What disciplinary procedures exist?

- To what extent is work efficiently organized?

- Could there be better ways of organizing the scarce resources in the workplace?

TASK 2

Arrange to interview a young worker, ideally in his or her place of work, so that you can experience at first hand the working environment of your interviewee. At the interview, make sure you note down carefully all the answers. You may prefer to tape the interview.

TASK 3

Write a 1000-word report listing your questions and summarizing the answers given.

Note: The report could be written on the basis of work experience you have had. You could write about your own experience of work and the working environment.

Dressing for the slopes

David Oates on ski outfitting from a Devonshire farmhouse

Disappointed that a broken leg prevented her from representing Britain in the 1968 Winter Olympics, Sue Jacoby sought consolation several years later by applying her ski-ing expertise to setting up a company in Devon.

South West Ski Wear, the firm she and her husband, Martin, run from a converted farm at Samford Peverell, near Tiverton, is coasting to healthy profits by providing a badly needed service in a growing market.

'I had tried to get some ski clothes for the children,' she said. 'We didn't want to pay the earth and ended up getting some stuff sent down from London. It was very tatty and thoroughly unsatisfactory. It only arrived two days before we were due to leave and there was panic as to whether the children would end up having any ski clothes at all.'

Sue suspected that others must be going through the same experience. There appeared to be an enticing hole in the market. She started her business modestly with a few anoraks and ski socks piled up in the spare bedroom, while the farm was still being renovated by Martin. 'It was chaotic and very unreal,' he recalls with a shudder.

The first year's turnover was a mere £1,000, but once the Jacobys made the breakthrough into the school market, they steadily built up to a turnover in excess of £50,000. At first it was only 10 schools, but it grew from year to year until the company could boast of more than 50 schools as customers. Business became so brisk that Martin decided to give up his teaching career and join Sue full time in the venture.

The couples' winning formula has been the personal service they provide, both to schools and to private customers. They deliver all the ski clothes personally to the schools and fit the children during their lunch-hour. Similarly, Sue thinks nothing of spending an hour-and-a-half fitting out a family of beginners in the firm's spacious showroom.

Martin doesn't disguise the fact that his familiarity with school life is of great value in building up business. In the months running up to the ski season, he can expect to spend five nights a week lecturing at parent evenings about the requirements of a successful ski holiday.

He is just as enthusiastic about the business. The first exercise he undertook after joining his wife in the venture was to contact 780 schools in the West country to find out which of them organised ski trips and were therefore a potential customer. He has festooned a large map of the South-west with 390 blue pins depicting the schools South West Ski Wear still has to win over as clients.

Most of their customers either pay in advance or on receipt, however, so their precarious financial position doesn't last long. 'We have no debt problems,' says Martin firmly. 'If a customer doesn't pay or a cheque bounces, they don't get anything from us.'

If the Jacoby's manage to win over just a fraction of the schools still to be conquered, finance is likely to be the least of their problems.

Source: The Guardian, 8 March 1985

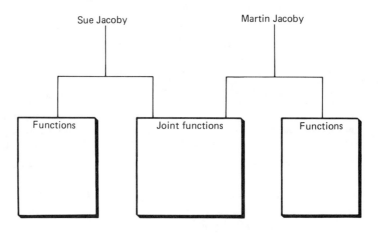

| Functions | Joint functions | Functions |

72

TASK

1 Briefly describe the business activity of South West Ski Wear.

2 State the tasks that are undertaken in the firm by (*a*) Sue Jacoby and (*b*) Martin Jacoby.

3 Draw an organizational chart showing the functions of Sue and Martin Jacoby as above. Where these functions are not clearly allocated in the article, make a guess at where you think the responsibility lies.

4 The company employs a secretary to deal with invoices. Show on the organizational chart to whom he or she would be responsible.

Poor pay blamed for big staff turnover

Low morale and poor pay grades may be responsible for a high turnover of staff in Sandwell's careers service, a report reveals. It says the number of staff leaving the department is causing concern.

Six of the borough's careers team of 20 changed jobs in the past year, four of them joining other authorities for more pay.

The report, to be discussed by the council's careers sub-committee on Wednesday, says there is a high turnover among staff which has led to a large number of probationary officers working in Sandwell.

'The combined effects of high turnover of staff, fewer promotion possibilities, cramped accommodation, high numbers of probationary careers officers as well as a very depressed labour market for jobs for young people in the borough all contribute to a lowering of morale,' says the report.

It adds: 'There is no one solution which will alleviate the problem of high turnover among careers officers.'

The report, drawn up by Sandwell's director of education Mr Gerald Brinsdon, says that in other West Midland authorities careers officers are on higher pay grades or have better promotion prospects.

Mr Brinsdon said that careers service inspectors had also criticised four of Sandwell's six careers centres as having cramped accommodation for staff which could contribute to the numbers leaving.

Source: Express and Star, 3 June 1985

TASK

1. Explain the nature of work of a careers office, both from the article and from your own contact with the Careers Advisory Service.

2. What were the poor working conditions described in the article and what was the effect of these?

3. Why are good working conditions essential for efficiency in work?

Low pay and sex torment for young

Working teenagers in the West Midlands have to endure sexual harassment, verbal abuse, unpaid overtime and dirty conditions—and wages as low as 48p an hour.

And they are the lucky ones because at least they have a job, according to a team investigating the plight of young workers.

A 16-year-old girl machinist complained that female staff were left in no doubt how they could find an extra £10 in their pay packet by an employer who regularly tried to touch her breast.

A 19-year-old clerk typist received just £25 for a 49-hour week, an 18-year-old with 11 O-Levels got £32.25 a week, while a young roofer was paid £6 for 12 hours overtime.

The examples of exploitation and abuse of teenage employees in a region with 15.3 per cent unemployment are contained in a report today from the West Midlands Low Pay Unit called Young Workers — the New Poor?

Cheap

It says the Young Workers Scheme and the Youth Training Scheme have been used to undermine Wages Council minimum rates

74

of pay and to create a supply of cheap labour for employers.

The results of government policies were likely to be a shortage of skilled workers and a generation of young people whose hopes, energy and enthusiasm had been crushed, said the unit.

It alleges that concentration on reducing young workers' wages is part of a wider strategy to reduce wages generally.

If young workers are cheap, they will often be in unfair competition with adult workers whose wages will fall too.

Source: Express and Star, 3 June 1985

TASK

1 What abuses in conditions of work were the Midlands Low Pay Unit complaining about?

2 Why do you think that employers are able to get away with these sorts of abuses, particularly with young people?

3 Why are poor conditions of work for young people likely to lead to poor conditions of work for adult workers too?

8 Trade unions

Approximately half of all workers in Britain are trade union members. Many more belong to professional associations and other organizations which perform many of the functions of trade unions. Despite this, trade unionism remains as controversial a topic as it has ever been. Why is this? Have trade unions a legitimate role to play in our economy? Would it be better if they were banned? In this chapter, the role of trade unions will be considered, as will their methods of work. Then some of the more controversial issues relating to trade unionism will be brought up in the assignments.

Functions

A trade union exists to defend the interests of its members in or out of work. This has a number of different aspects. Firstly, a trade union exists to defend workers' interests against their employers. Employers vary, from a local self-employed man or woman who hires one worker, to the government which has millions of workers on its payroll, and from companies whose major goal is to make profits, to a trade union itself whose aim is to defend the interests of workers. Employers have power over the workers they employ. They can hire and fire workers, fix their level of pay, and determine their working conditions. The larger the organization, the more difficult it is for one worker to make his views known to those with the power to implement change. Also, the larger the organization, the less influence any single worker can have on how it is run. With a bad employer, this can result in the exploitation of workers. The employer can use the weakness of unorganized labour to pay low wages and inflict poor working conditions on workers, and then use the money gained to boost profits. It is for this reason that trade unions have come to be an essential part of every industrial democracy in the world today. By uniting together, workers can increase their power in the workplace and have a chance to defend themselves against employers whose main aims are likely to conflict with the aims of their workers.

Exercise

What disputes between workers and companies are in the news at the moment? Write a short paragraph describing one dispute and say how you think it will end.

Government's role

Not only employers but governments too can greatly influence the lives of workers. For instance, in the UK, working conditions are regulated by a large number of laws designed to protect workers in their working environment. Laws relating to sickness benefit, industrial injuries benefit, unemployment benefit and pensions are obviously of vital interest to the ordinary worker. So too are government policies which might affect whether or not a worker's job will continue to exist in the future. A decision by government to cut aid to the textile industry or allow more imports of textiles or simply to increase taxes, thus reducing the purchasing power of ordinary consumers, will be of vital interest to a worker employed by a textile company. The government also sets the boundaries within which trade unions can work. It has the power to change existing laws thereby reducing or increasing the power of trade unions in the everyday world. In doing this, the government is of course reducing or increasing the power of ordinary workers in their places of work up and down the country.

Exercise

Find a current item of news which relates to the government and workers. Summarize what is happening and justify whether or not you agree with the government's position.

Monetary benefits

A third way in which trade unions have traditionally protected their members' interests is by organizing a variety of schemes which provide monetary benefits to members. With the growth of the welfare state in the UK, the importance of these benefits has declined. However, a union may provide cash benefit for illness, unemployment, retirement, injury at work and even, in one or two cases, private health care.

Organization

To those outside, it can often seem as though a trade union has an individual mind and will. This is not the case. A trade union is a democratic body and its actions are guided by the decisions of its members. There are both official channels of organization and unofficial ones.

Each union has its own particular organization but most are very similar. The organization starts at the bottom, with ordinary members on the 'shop floor'—the place of work of a member. Members elect representatives—often called shop stewards. A shop steward is responsible for representing his or her workers' interests to their employers and within the union organization. Shop stewards will meet on a day-to-day basis with management to deal with problems as they arise. In larger companies or organizations, this means dealing with the personnel officer, who is the member of management appointed by the employers to deal

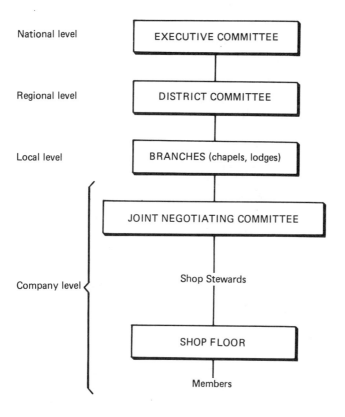

specifically with workers and their problems. Larger issues, such as pay rises, are likely to be dealt with by a special committee called by different names in different organizations, but here we will use the term 'joint negotiating committee'. Collective bargaining now takes place, because the workers and the employers group together or act collectively to appoint representatives to defend their interests on the joint negotiating committee. In smaller establishments, all shop stewards will sit on this committee while in larger organizations, only some will represent all their members.

The trade union will be organized at a local level into a branch (or 'chapel' or 'lodge'). If the employer is very large, then all the shop floor worker members of a branch may work for just the one employer. More usually, a branch is made up of workers from several different places of work and different employers. A branch will discuss issues of local and national interest and all individual members of the branch are entitled to attend meetings, speak and vote on the issues under discussion.

Branches may be organized in a regional organization run by a 'district committee'. For instance, the Westminster branch may be represented by the London and South East district committee of the union. At the top of the trade union, will be the 'executive committee'—representing the union at national level. Some of the presidents or secretaries of these national executive committees are household names, people like Ron Todd and Arthur Scargill.

Much of the work of a trade union is done by unpaid officials like shop stewards, who also work full-time at an ordinary job. However, full-time trade union officials paid for out of members' union subscriptions are equally vital for the efficient working of a union. A full-time official is able to build up a much greater knowledge of government legislation, union organization, workers' rights, education and training opportunities, etc. than unpaid part-time officials. There will almost certainly be full-time officials working at the head office of the union and, indeed, all the members of the executive committee are likely to be full-time paid officials; some may also be attached to a branch or district.

Trade union officials are servants of the ordinary members of the union. It is their job to listen to what members are saying and to carry out their instructions. The ultimate power is not the executive committee but the Annual Conference of the union. Delegates are elected by ordinary shop floor members and the conference has the power to pass resolutions which are then binding on the union and its executive. If a trade union leader were to carry out policies which the conference disapproved of, then it has the power to overturn those policies and to sack the official. This happens very rarely because officials do listen to what their members say and try to carry out those policies to the best of their ability.

Shop stewards, district committees, etc. form part of the official means of communication and organization of the union. But there are very important unofficial channels. Newspapers often talk about 'Mr X' bringing 'his members' out on strike, as if a union leader had the power to decide upon a strike by himself. This simply isn't true. Shop floor workers often go out on strike despite their union leaders saying they should stay at work—these are often called 'unofficial' strikes. Equally, shop stewards and other union officials may call members out on strike but the workers can carry on working. Ordinary workers have a mind of their own: it is their pay packets and conditions of work which are affected by industrial action. And because so much is at stake, although members listen to the advice that their union gives them, they are often prepared to reject it.

Exercise

Make a list of all the trade unions that you can think of. If possible, name the top official of each union.

Methods of work

The popular image of a trade union is that it is an organization that exists to bring its members out on strike. This is far from the truth. Nearly all disputes between trade unions and employers are resolved peacefully through negotiations. Talking round problems and finding a peaceful solution is the bread and butter work of a union. Negotiation, not confrontation, is the typical scene in British Industrial relations.

In the very rare instances when industrial action is taken, trade unions have a variety of courses of action open to them. They can, of course, come out on strike, but this is a very costly solution for the workers involved, and also for their union if the workers have to be given strike pay. Limited action is likely to be preferred at the start of a dispute. This could include measures such as a one-day strike (a 'token' strike), a work-to-rule (where workers will only do work which is specified in their contract of employment), or an overtime ban.

Management too can resort to industrial action. They can try to suspend or sack individual workers (although this is difficult given the tight laws now surrounding dismissal and disciplining of workers) or they can lock workers out—that is, not allow workers to come to work.

Negotiation is, however, by far the most important way in which disputes are resolved, and will continue to be so in the future.

Important points to keep in mind

1. **A majority of workers belong to trade unions and professional associations.**

2. **These exist to protect the interest of their members—against their employers, against government and at times against their fellow workers.**

3. **A trade union is a democratic body. Most unions have a mixture of full-time staff, some elected into office, some not, and unpaid officers who are almost all elected into office.**

4. **Nearly all disputes in which trade unions are involved are resolved peacefully. Only in a very small fraction of cases is there recourse to industrial action.**

Industrial relations

This project will not only teach you the meanings of terms related to industrial relations, but it will also help you develop research skills.

80

TASK

Use a library (your school or college library, or a public library) to find out and write down the meaning of the following:

wage differentials	shop steward
collective bargaining	union convenor
closed shop	branch
chapel	picket
strike ballot	national executive
go slow	white-collar union
lock out	selective strike
unfair dismissal	Tolpuddle Martyrs
craft union	work to rule
shop floor members	general trade union
trade union conference	unofficial strike
industrial action	blacking
scabs	victimization
industrial union	TUC
professional association	ACAS

Sayonara to strife, strikes and shop stewards

By James McMillan

Yokoso, Nippon . . . welcome, Japan
The Great Copier has become the Great Innovator, in the vital area where we British do worst of all—industrial relations.

It has been left to Nissan, makers of Datsun cars, to conclude a single union agreement with a British trade union.

Only the Amalgamated Union of Engineering Workers will operate in Nissan's Wearside factory. In return, the union has agreed to arbitration, craft flexibility and no shop stewards.

Glory, be! No shop stewards! At a car plant? It's like Old Lace without the Arsenic.

Their place will be taken by shop-floor representatives who will sit on a company council.

Impact
Mr Peter Wickens, Nissan's personnel director, says there is no such thing as a no-

strike agreement that will stick. That's as maybe.

He is clearly putting his trust in creating conditions where calling a strike would be virtually unthinkable. And where the principle of 'mucking in' together will have taken such firm root as to eliminate practically every dispute.

In addition, foremen will be replaced with supervisors, paid £12,500 a year to ensure quality control.

Thus, by buying the rule book—paying such good money that first-class work is assured—Nissan hopes to transform grievance-hunters into bounty-hunters.

Smart. This transformation in working practices (including one uniform and one canteen for everyone) is bound to have a profound impact on the British labour scene.

Take arbitration: Instead of splitting the conflicting claims of union and management down the middle, the referee will choose one or other; thereby encouraging moderation in pay demands and fairness in management response. The two sides will move naturally towards the central ground.

Still more significantly, workers will not be obliged to be members of the AUEW. They will be encouraged to join, but they will not be obliged to do so.

Doing away with the closed shop will greatly strengthen the company's ability to meet new challenges and to compete with maximum competence and elasticity.

If Nissan's methods achieve startling productivity and pay rises—and if Nissan is followed by Honda, as it very well may be—how long will it be before the workers at BL, Ford and Talbot start clamouring for similar deals?

This could be the real Workers' Revolution for People's Capitalism, Japanese-style.

Source: *Daily Express*, 24 April 1985

81

TASK

1 Nissan is to set up a new car plant in Wearside in the North East of England. What do Nissan make?

2 What is meant by a 'single union agreement'?

3 Explain three ways in which this agreement is different from what is usual in British industrial relations.

4 What is the role of a shop steward in a normal factory?

5 Why should 'craft flexibility' increase worker productivity?

6 Why might workers at other car companies in Britain 'start clamouring for similar deals'?

Post union's stamp of disapproval

by Richard Brooks

Britain's postal workers are edging nearer a strike following the break-down of talks between the Union of Communications Workers (UCW) and the Post Office last week. The sticking points are the PO's wish to increase part-time workers from 8,500 to 20,000, its plans to get all 120,000 workers to join a compulsory productivity system, and the introduction of more mechanical sorting.

'These major reforms in working practices are too important to be dropped, if agreement with the union cannot be obtained,' says PO chairman Sir Ron Dearing. The UCW counters by saying that a special conference this month was firmly opposed to manpower cuts, and any increase in part-timers.

The postal workers are taking a tough stand. They believe they have already improved the mail service, and do not want to sacrifice jobs.

The PO, on the other hand, feels that productivity and the volume of mail handled, particularly parcels cannot be improved without fundamental restructuring. It is anxious to improve the reliability of the service, which is still below par.

It would rather not increase the price of stamps and would prefer to reverse the falling trend in turnover and profits with a more cost-efficient service.

At present 56% of the postal workers have joined the voluntary productivity scheme. The PO wants it to become compulsory. It also wants workers to accept a move away from voluntary to guaranteed overtime, which should ideally be worked between 7am and 9am, and between 5.30pm and 7pm. About 70% of the mail is posted after 5pm.

In return for an agreement the Post Office will offer no compulsory redundancies, a boost in earnings of between 5% and 10% on the average £150-a-week

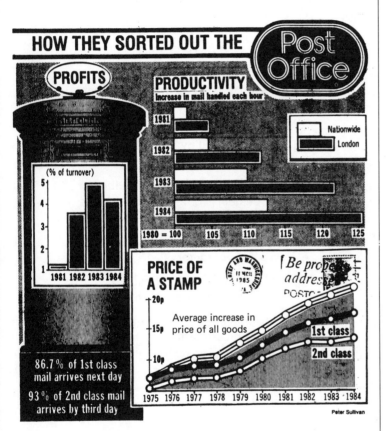

HOW THEY SORTED OUT THE Post Office

PROFITS

(% of turnover)

5 — 4 — 3 — 2 — 1 —

1981 1982 1983 1984

PRODUCTIVITY
increase in mail handled each hour

1981
1982
1983
1984

1980 = 100   105   110   115   120   125

☐ Nationwide
■ London

86.7% of 1st class mail arrives next day

93% of 2nd class mail arrives by third day

PRICE OF A STAMP

20p
15p
10p

Average increase in price of all goods

1st class
2nd class

1975 1976 1977 1978 1979 1980 1981 1982 1983 1984

Be prope addres POST...

Peter Sullivan

earnings, and a share in the net savings from the introduction of new machine sorting equipment.

The amount of mail being handled by postal workers has gone up considerably in the past three years. The biggest increase is in parcels, which is expected to rise to about 205m items sent in the year ending March 31. In the year to March 1981, 172m parcels were sent.

The Post Office itself is very keen to get more of the public to use the postal code.

Source: Sunday Times, 17 March 1985

TASK 1

Together with three or four other people, **either** research an industrial relations dispute currently taking place (each person should write a short report explaining the causes of the dispute and how it has developed) **or** prepare your report about the postal dispute.

TASK 2

Half the group should now take the trade union side and half the management. Act out negotiations to resolve the dispute. Then write a short report describing those negotiations and how the dispute was resolved.

Jobcentre staff in walkout over cuts

By Carson Black

Hundreds of Midland civil servants walked out on strike yesterday in protest at planned cuts to Jobcentres.

The protest came as the Manpower Services Commission approved the economies.

Offices in Solihull, central Birmingham and Erdington were closed early yesterday and were followed by others in Coventry, Handsworth and Small Heath in the afternoon.

The MSC plans to increase the number of Jobcentres in the country but reduce the service they provide — a move that will lead to 500 job losses.

Intolerable

Yesterday's spontaneous industrial action could lead to a rolling programme of strikes and disruptive action by the two big civil service unions.

Civil and Public Services Association official Mr Keith Brown, said: 'These plans will severely limit the service we provide to the public. It will especially hit the long-term unemployed because there will no longer be any personal counselling services provided and it is our experience that it is these long term unemployed who need that type of service most.

'The job losses are also intolerable because we have already suffered severe cutbacks in the past three or four years.'

There are 130 Jobcentres across the Midlands but the cuts are likely to affect the inner city offices most.

The executive bodies of both the CPSA and the Society of Civil and Public Servants, representing the majority of civil servants in the Jobcentres, are to discuss the MSC plans in the New Year.

Source: The Birmingham Post, 15 December 1984

TASK

1 What was the cause of the strike?

2 What does it mean when it says that the strike was 'spontaneous'?

3 Why does the Civil and Public Services Association feel that an increase in the number of Jobcentres in the country will lead to a reduction in services?

4 Do you think that the civil servants were right to go on strike? Explain your answer carefully.

Industrial stoppages

Total working days lost (Thousands)

	Workers involved	All industries and services	Coal, coke, mineral oil and natural gas	Metals, engineering, and vehicles	Textiles, footwear and clothing	Construction	Transport and communication	All other industries and services
1982	2 101	5 313	380	1 457	61	41	1 675	1 699
1983	573	3 754	591	1 420	32	68	295	1 348
1984	1 375	26 564	22 265	2 024	64	93	660	1 458

Source: CSO, *Monthly Digest of Statistics*, March 1985

TASK

1 How many workers went on strike in (a) 1982 and (b) 1984?

2 Twenty workers went on strike for 2 days. How many working days were lost in the dispute?

3 100 working days were lost where 50 workers went on strike. How long were they on strike for?

4 Estimate the average length in days of a strike in (a) 1982, (b) 1983 and (c) 1984.

5 In which of the three years was there (a) least strike activity and (b) most strike activity?

6 Draw a bar chart showing the breakdown by industry of working days lost through strikes in 1984.

7 Explain why the number of working days lost increased seven-fold between 1983 and 1984, while the number of workers involved only increased 2½ times.

THE CLOSED SHOP DEBATE

John Lloyd *Labour Correspondent*

The argument over the closed shop is one between two principles which are promoted by their supporters as moral absolutes: individual liberty versus common solidarity.

Nowhere has the clash of these principles been clearer than in the town of Walsall.

In July, 1980, two months after the election of a Labour council the new council signed a union membership, or closed shop, agreement with its manual unions.

Letters from the unions went out to all council manual workers.

At least seven of the staff immediately determined that they would not join. Over the next few months, two of these were to change their minds. Another, a member of the Plymouth Brethren sect, was excused.

The remaining four—Mrs Wendy Clifft, Mrs Gloria Price, Mrs Irene Russell and Mrs Doris Todd—all opposed unions generally on political grounds. Mrs Todd says: 'I just felt I didn't want to join Nupe. There are some unions that are all right and some that are not all right.'

Mrs Todd, a 36-year-old former Wren, is strong-willed and, on occasion, outspoken. A photograph of members of the Royal Family is on a shelf of her immaculate council maisonette in the Birmingham suburb of Erdington.

She worked with 16 other women at Streetly comprehensive where she made no secret of her refusal to join Nupe, National Union of Public Employees. One day, she says, she was summoned to the phone to speak to the Nupe kitchen staff organiser. 'You have no alternative but to join,' she told her.

Referring to a little diary in which she has logged events, Mrs Todd went on: 'On the 18th of September some weeks after that I was working away. The organiser came into the kitchen. She told me: "You're going to get the sack for not joining a union. Why don't you join." I said to her: "You are not my boss. I read in the papers that Alan Fisher (the Nupe general secretary) gave £3,000 to the Morning Star and I'm not joining that kind of set-up."' (Nupe does not usually make donations of this kind. This one was in recognition of the paper's coverage of the union during the public service strikes of the winter of 1978-79.)

The organiser for the school meals staff is Mrs Doreen Bottomley whose husband, Mr Ed Bottomley is the full-time Nupe official for the area. The two women still display a lively dislike of each other: not suprisingly—Mrs Bottomley, like Mrs Todd, is strong-willed and a straight talker.

'My feeling about these particular ladies is this: if they've got such strong conscientious objections to joining a union why take advantage of the wage rises and improved conditions the union has won,' says Mrs Bottomley.

Mrs Irene Russell, however thought little about unions except that they were too powerful.

Her opposition to joining was strengthened the more they tried to persuade her to join. 'I just got stubborn and said, why should I?'

The four women were all told to appear before a disputes panel at the town hall in the first few months of 1981. Their reasons for refusing to join were judged inadequate.

Mrs Todd had written a letter to the panel which was read out in her presence. In it, she accused the council of wishing to see 'the hammer and sickle above the town hall.'

The women were given notice—during which period they could join the union and keep their jobs. None did. Consequently, they lost their jobs.

Source: Financial Times, 29 January 1982

TASK

1 What is a 'closed shop'?

2 How many workers finally refused to join the Walsall closed shop?

3 What did Walsall decide to do when these workers refused to join?

4 Explain carefully why Mrs Todd and Mrs Russell refused to join a union.

5 Explain why Mrs Bottomley thought that they should join a union.

6 Which side do you think was right in this dispute? Explain your answer carefully.

Union operation

This project will help you to investigate the roles and methods of operation of a particular trade union or professional association.

TASK 1

Identify a particular place of work which you wish to investigate. You may choose on the basis that a relative or a friend works there and can help make the right contacts; or you may work there yourself on a part-time basis; or you may choose the school or college where you study; or you may wish to obtain a job there or in a similar establishment. It should be sufficiently large to have a union representative (shop stewards or equivalent). Make contact with a union representative—by personal approach, by letter or telephone, or through an intermediary—and arrange to conduct an interview. Explain, when arranging the interview, that you wish to investigate the role and methods of operation of the trade union in that place of work.

TASK 2

Draw up a list of questions to ask in the interview. It should include some about the role of the trade union such as:

◆ Why does the trade union need to defend the rights of workers in the face of employers?

◆ Why does the trade union need to monitor the activities of government?

◆ Why does the trade union need to provide benefits such as insurance for members?

The list should also include questions about the methods of operation of the union such as:

◆ How many union representatives are there in the place of work? How many union members do they represent? What do the union representatives do?

◆ How does the union organization at the place of work link in to the wider pattern of union activities?

◆ What channels of communication exist between unions and employers?

TASK 3

Conduct the interview. Make notes on the answers given. You may prefer to tape the interview, but you must ask the permission of the interviewee for this beforehand. Do not be afraid to ask supplementary questions to the ones you have written down; nor to ask the interviewee to explain any point you may not have understood.

TASK 4

Write a 2000-word report on 'the roles and methods of operation of a trade union/professional association'.

9 A lifetime of working

Which path to take

Look at the chart. Where are you now? What path do you think you will follow through life? What path would you like to follow? Can you make any plans today about what you will be doing in ten, thirty or fifty years' time, given the current state of the job market? Nearly everyone starts off life by attending school, which should provide basic academic skills, such as 'the 3 Rs' (reading, writing and arithmetic), social skills (being able to work with others) as well as providing more advanced skills in a variety of subject areas such as economics or French. Qualifications such as GCSEs or CPVEs are just one way of indicating how well an individual has done at school.

After school, a pupil may decide to stay on in further or higher education in order to further his or her personal development. A few may go directly into a job. Many more will join work experience and training schemes such as the Youth Training Scheme before going into full-time work or joining the dole queue. Only some workers can expect to spend all of their working lives in a full-time job. Many women leave employment to bring up a family and when they go back to work, it may well be on a part-time basis. Some workers can expect to stay in the same job for a lifetime and a change of jobs may well involve retraining. You may feel excited by all this, or it may all be very frightening. What factors will affect your progress through your working life?

Exercise

Consider the flow chart. What path do you see yourself taking through life? Why do you expect it to be like this?

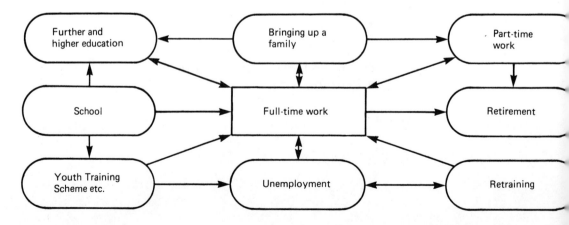

Careers advice

One major factor which will affect your progress is you yourself and the decisions you make. Before making an important decision, it is essential to have as much information as possible of relevance to the making of that decision.

Let's assume, for instance, that you are now at school or college. You want to leave at the end of the year and get a full-time job. If you are to make the best decision, you will need to find out:

◆ what jobs are likely to be available

◆ whether or not you have the right qualifications and experience

◆ how to apply for them successfully

◆ and last but not least, how well you think you will like doing a particular job

Put another way, you need careers advice, and this is available from a number of sources. First of all, ask your parents, older brothers and sisters, other relations, friends of the family. They have a good knowledge of their own occupations and the chances are that you will be considering applying for the sort of job that your family knows something about.

Go to your library, either the school or college library or the public library, and read up about jobs you are thinking of applying for. There is often a large range of reading material—books, pamphlets, leaflets—which can be consulted.

Your local Careers Advisory Service is there specifically to serve you and give young people careers advice. Careers officers regularly visit schools and colleges; they will interview you and help you make your job choice. Later on in life, your local Jobcentre will provide the same service for you.

Exercise

What careers advice have you had so far and from whom? How could you make better use of the careers guidance facilities available to you?

Career progression

Progress in a career can mean different things to different people. For many, it means gaining promotion—more money and more responsibility. For others, it means moving to a job which is very satisfying but does not necessarily give more money. And there are others for whom it means earning enough money to be able to afford to retire or go into semi-retirement.

Remember, economics is the study of how scarce resources are allocated. Your time and talents are a scarce resource and you have a choice about how these should be allocated. Equally, you do not have a completely free choice. Not everyone can become a brain surgeon or Prime Minister, however much they might want to. What are the constraints in a market economy on an individual's freedom of choice of occupation?

Experience and qualifications are one obvious constraint. In general, the more experience and qualifications that can be gained in the early part of a working life, the more occupational and promotional opportunities there will be for an individual. This is because education and work experience make a worker more versatile, more adaptable, and more capable of performing a particular task. The further one goes up an organization, the more qualifications and the more experience will be demanded of the successful applicant.

Exercise

Find out (for instance from your school or college careers library) the minimum entry requirements for SRN nursing and a police cadet.

Economic climate

Another constraint is the economic climate in a particular market or in the economy as a whole. Since the mid-1970s, it has been relatively easy to make a quick career progression in computing because this is an up-and-coming profession or industry. The demand for suitably qualified workers has tended to outstrip supply, giving rise to high wages and excellent career prospects. The same has not been true of teaching: since the mid-1970s, with the number of children in schools declining and governments anxious to cut back spending, pay and promotion prospects have been very poor; moreover, many who have trained to become teachers have found it difficult to get jobs. In a declining industry such as shipbuilding, the situation has been even worse. Since the mid-1970s (and before); shipbuilding workers have not only been faced with poor prospects but, due to foreign competition and a slack market for new ships worldwide, they have had to face the serious prospect of redundancy. In general, it is much harder to get a job today than it was twenty or even ten years ago because the economy has not been able to provide sufficient jobs for all those who want them.

Exercise

Obtain a copy of your local newspaper and turn to the 'Job vacancies' advertisement section. For each advertisement, state what industry the job is in. Are these industries expanding or declining?

Other influences

Where you live is also vital to your career prospects. If you live in the south-east of England, job prospects are much better than if you live in Liverpool, Glasgow or Belfast. Your chances of getting a job and gaining promotion are much better if you are able and prepared to move round the country.

You yourself will greatly influence your career progress. The energy with which you pursue career aims will help or hinder progress as the case may be. The 16-year-old who writes letters to 100 local firms asking for job opportunities is far more likely to get a job than the one who does nothing about getting a job when he or she leaves school.

Other factors, such as luck or discrimination, should also not be ignored. It is often said that those who make it to the top of their profession had the 'right break' or were 'in the right place at the right time'. Discrimination may act in your favour or against you. In our society today, a large number of groups are discriminated against. You will find it harder to get a job if you are under 25, over 40, black, female, handicapped, working class or have the 'wrong' regional accent, for instance. It is, of course, illegal for an employer to discriminate against any worker or any applicant for a job, but this is so difficult to prove that the law is often ignored.

Exercise

Have you ever suffered from discrimination? Do you think it is right that discrimination should exist in jobs? Explain your answer carefully.

Obtaining a job

Getting a job is not always easy in an economy where there are at least 3 million people unemployed. There are, however, ways in which it is possible to improve your chances of obtaining employment.

Always maintain an active job search. Frequent visits to the Careers Advisory Service or the Jobcentre, constant enquiries among family, friends and neighbours, and looking at local and national newspaper job adverts every day is only common sense.

Try not to remain unemployed for any length of time. Evidence suggests that the longer you have been out of work the more likely it is that you will remain unemployed. In part, this is because employers prefer to employ a worker 'who has had recent experience of work and is familiar with routines and procedures'. The longer you stay unemployed, the more will your skills and talents become obsolete. This means that it is better to accept a placement on a government training scheme than stay at home doing nothing, even if you feel that the training scheme is very poor and that you are gaining no personal benefit from it. It means that undertaking voluntary work is useful for getting a paid job later. Or you may consider self-employment where working is more important than making a large profit. With 3 million unemployed, there aren't enough jobs for everybody who wants one. It's a sad fact of life that if you want a job you've got to appear better to an employer than somebody else. The choice of whether or not to compete in the job market is yours.

92   *Exercise*   Have you tried to get a job? If so, how did you set about it and what success did you have? If not, find out how friends or relatives obtained their present job.

Important points to keep in mind

1. You are most unlikely to stay in the same job all your life. You need to be prepared for change.

2. Good careers advice is essential if you are to make the right decision about a career.

3. How well you get on in a career is dependent upon your qualifications, your experience, your competence and your energy as well as external factors such as the strength of industry, luck and discrimination.

4. Obtaining a job is often not easy but maintaining an active search is essential and so is flexibility in choice of jobs.

Which way?

TASK

Choose one of these careers and state which route you would want to take if you were entering them. Explain carefully why you would want to take that particular route.

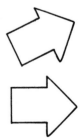

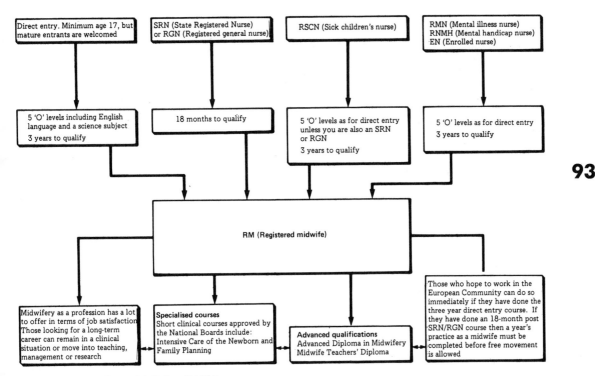

Direct entry. Minimum age 17, but mature entrants are welcomed	SRN (State Registered Nurse) or RGN (Registered general nurse)	RSCN (Sick children's nurse)	RMN (Mental illness nurse) RNMH (Mental handicap nurse) EN (Enrolled nurse)
5 'O' levels including English language and a science subject 3 years to qualify	18 months to qualify	5 'O' levels as for direct entry unless you are also an SRN or RGN 3 years to qualify	5 'O' levels as for direct entry 3 years to qualify

RM (Registered midwife)

Midwifery as a profession has a lot to offer in terms of job satisfaction. Those looking for a long-term career can remain in a clinical situation or move into teaching, management or research

Specialised courses
Short clinical courses approved by the National Boards include: Intensive Care of the Newborn and Family Planning

Advanced qualifications
Advanced Diploma in Midwifery
Midwife Teachers' Diploma

Those who hope to work in the European Community can do so immediately if they have done the three year direct entry course. If they have done an 18-month post SRN/RGN course then a year's practice as a midwife must be completed before free movement is allowed

Source: Midwifery, CSO for DHSS

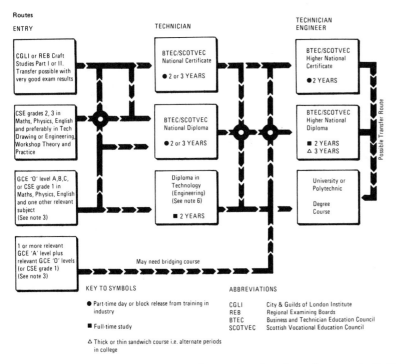

Source: Engineering Careers Information Service, *Careers in British Engineering*

94

Opportunities for Technically-minded young people

For those interested in the technology of broadcasting the BBC can offer unrivalled prospects.

This year a number of vacancies exist for young people to train as Engineers working throughout the UK. In order for an application to be successful you will need to possess good 'O' Level passes in English, Maths and Physics and to have studied to examination standard in 'A' Level Maths and Physics. Alternatively we will consider TEC Diplomas in a suitable Electronics-based subject. Successful applicants will also have a strong practical proven interest in a relevant subject such as Hi-Fi, amateur electronics or home video. In addition there are a limited number of vacancies in our Operational Department for Camera Operators and Audio Assistants; here above all, your interests will be of sufficient depth to discuss technicalities of photography and sound. A good standard of literacy and numeracy will be required and typically will include 'O' Level passes in English, Maths and Physics. As all posts are in Operational areas a minimum age of 18 is necessary plus normal hearing and colour vision.

For further details and application form please write to The Engineering Recruitment Officer, BBC, Broadcasting House, P.O. Box 2BL, London W1A 2BL, quoting reference no. 85.E.4022/DM and enclosing an s.a.e. measuring at least 9" × 5".

We are an equal opportunities employer.

Source: Daily Mail, 24 April 1985

TASK

1. What qualifications do you need to become a BBC engineer?

2. What qualifications do you need to become a Camera Operator and Audio Assistant?

3. What experience do you need in order to obtain either of the jobs advertised?

4. If you were hard of hearing, how would this affect your chances of getting the jobs in the advertisement?

Interviews

This project is designed to give you skills in interviewing as well as knowledge of an individual's career progression.

TASK 1

You will be interviewing an individual worker about his or her career progression to date. Draw up a list of questions which will help you write an account of that worker's progression in his or her job and why that particular progression occurred. Among other matters, you will need to find out what jobs your interviewee has had, what his or her qualifications are and when they were obtained, how did he or she obtain particular jobs, what has influenced the way in which his or her career has progressed and how he or she views career progression in the future.

TASK 2

Choose two or more adult workers to interview. They may be family, friends of the family or other workers you know. When you first approach them, ask them politely whether or not they would be prepared to be interviewed, outline the nature of the questions to be asked and the reasons why you wish to conduct an interview. Fix a time and a place for the interview. During the interview, note down the answers given to your questions. Alternatively, you may prefer to tape the interview, but you must ask permission of the interviewee first. Do not be afraid to ask questions which are not on your initial list, nor to ask for clarification if you don't understand the answer to a particular question. Thank the interviewee for his or her help.

TASK 3

Write a 500-word report on each of the people you interviewed. Then write a 250-word conclusion comparing how they have progressed.

This project requires you to use a careers library. Research a career progression for a career that you are interested in. In particular, find out how to enter that career, what qualifications or experience are desirable or essential, and what progression there is. Also, assess the monetary rewards offered in the career as well as the job satisfaction likely to be obtained.

TASK

Write up your findings in the form of a 1000-word report.

Job suitability

Craftsmen

SOLIHULL

British Gas has vacancies for experienced Craftsmen to work at the Midlands Research Station at Solihull

Rigger/Slinger

To work primarily as part of a small team engaged in a wide variety of slinging, rigging and lifting work

Applicants should have a good working knowledge of current legislation relating to inspection and maintenance of lifting equipment and should also possess a current full driving licence. Reference number MRS/513

Pipefitter

To work on the construction and maintenance of pressurised chemical plant and services.

Applicants should have working knowledge of high pressure piped systems with ideally a petrochemical background. Reference numberMRS/516

A degree of flexibility is expected from both positions embracing other craft skills as well as the main duties.

All applicants should have served recognised apprenticeships with related academic qualifications and at least three years relevant experience.

Both posts, open to men and women equally, carry staff status and are designated Senior Technicians under the Research Station staff structure

Write for application forms quoting the appropriate reference number (see above) to: Senior Personnel Officer, British Gas Corporation, Midlands Research Station, Wharf Lane, Solihull, West Midlands

BRITISH GAS

Source: The Birmingham Post, 15 December 1984

TASK

1 What academic qualifications do each of the jobs require?

2 What experience is required of a successful applicant?

3 What does it mean when it says that 'a degree of flexibility is expected from both positions'?

4 Why is it unlikely that many women will apply for these jobs?

Is this for me?

Source: Daily Mail, 24 April 1985

CUSTOMER & PRODUCT SUPPORT–HARDWARE & SOFTWARE

Why take a shot in the dark
when we can put some light into your future.

At Prime Computer, we've been taking an innovative stand on customer and product support since our inception over 12 years ago demonstrating an exceptional commitment to this area. With a U.K. turnover in excess of £50m and an enviable reputation for product excellence and technical support in the super mini league, we have reinforced our strategy with the establishment of a national customer support centre at Hayes, Middlesex.

We are now seeking high calibre and particularly self motivated software and hardware engineers with the determination and enthusiasm to join our Product and Customer Support groups.

Product Support

We take new products and ensure their smooth introduction to our customer base, ensuring they meet our customers' needs and our high standards of serviceability. You'll need five years' experience in a manufacturer, major systems builder or software house

INFORMAL INTERVIEWS
Come along to the HEATHROW POST HOUSE HOTEL, Heathrow Airport, on Thursday 25th April between noon and 9 pm and we'll put some light into your future. If you can't make it, drop us a line with your career history to, or telephone, Chris Verney, Human Resources Manager, Prime Computer (UK) Ltd., Primos House, Lampton Road, Hounslow, Middlesex. Telephone 01-572 7400

Heathrow Post House Hotel

First and Foremost

combined with an enquiring, pragmatic but innovative approach.

Customer Support

The central role to our technical support function we provide solutions to customer queries covering a wide range of applications. We need software engineers with at least five years' experience in a major systems house, systems builder or a manufacturer in the mini or mainframe field. The ability to trouble shoot and debug systems backed up by experience of COMMS,

DBMS, or DMS is essential.

At this stage, we're just asking you to come and talk to us without any commitment. You'll find that at Prime, support roles command exceptional future potential. We'll show you how our training and career development has a well deserved reputation for being first class. On top of that there's a comprehensive benefits package that's bound to put a light in your eye. Top salaries are backed up by a preferential share scheme, company car, free BUPA and pension and life assurance schemes.

PRIME PRIME PRIME PRIME PRIME PRIME **PR1ME** PRIME PRIME PRIME PRIME PRIME PRIME

Computer

TASK

1. What is the job being advertised?

2. Describe the company which is advertising for new workers.

3. Explain what is meant in the advertisement by:
   - 'high calibre and particularly self motivated' workers
   - 'an enquiring, pragmatic but innovative approach'
   - 'ability to trouble shoot and debug systems'
   - 'exceptional future potential'
   - 'training and career development'
   - 'comprehensive benefits package'

4. How would you set about trying to work for Prime Computer (UK) Limited?

Percentage unemployment by region

(1st Quarter of Each Year, Seasonally Adjusted)

	1965 %	1975 %	1985 %
North	2.5	4.9	19.1
Yorkshire and Humberside	1.0	3.0	15.1
East Midlands	0.7	2.7	12.9
East Anglia	1.2	2.6	10.9
South east	0.8	2.0	10.3
South west	1.4	3.5	12.7
West Midlands	0.6	2.7	15.7
North west	1.6	4.1	16.7
Wales	2.3	4.2	17.4
Scotland	3.0	4.2	16.1
Northern Ireland	5.9	5.8	21.3
United Kingdom	1.4	3.1	13.7

Source: CSO, Economic Trends

TASK

1. Which area had the lowest percentage unemployment in (a) 1965, (b) 1975 and (c) 1985?

2. Which area has had the highest percentage unemployment over the period?

3. Percentage unemployment increased about ten-fold over the period 1965 to 1985 in the north-west. How many times did percentage unemployment increase in each of the other regions in the UK? Rank order the regions in terms of the increase in percentage unemployment, putting the highest at the top.

4. If you were an unskilled unemployed worker and prepared to move anywhere in the country to look for a job, which regions would you have gone to in (a) 1965, (b) 1975 and (c) 1985. Which regions would you have avoided in these three years?

5. Give **two** reasons why unemployment varies between regions.

6. Why can the region in which you live have a serious affect on your career prospects?

10 Businesses

The most important function of a business in an economy is the production of goods and services. In a **planned economy**, like that of the USSR, businesses are mostly state-owned. It is the government which owns most firms and decides what is to be produced, how it is produced and how products are to be allocated among consumers. In a **mixed economy** like the UK's, a mixture of state organizations and firms—such as the National Health Service and the National Coal Board—and privately owned firms organize production. This chapter will consider how the second of these, privately owned businesses, function.

The product

Private businesses exist to produce goods and services which are sold in the market place. The decision as to what to sell can be simple, or very complicated. Take, for example, a window cleaner: he only has to decide what services he will offer as a window cleaner and where he will offer these services. Given that there are only a few different types of 'washes' possible and that a local area is fairly small, his decisions are relatively simple to make.

For a large company, however, the decision-making process is far more complicated. A new product may cost millions of pounds to develop and launch and the very survival of the firm may be at stake. In these circumstances, a firm is likely to engage in **market research**, the process by which a firm tries to find out what products and what features of those products will tempt consumers to buy. There are a variety of ways in which a firm can test consumers' opinions. Firstly, firms can investigate the size of the market and potential sales by looking at the large number of statistics available. For instance, a publishing firm might want to set up a new magazine aimed at teenage boys aged 13 to 17. Some basic desk research would quickly establish the number of boys aged 13 to 17 in the UK today and this would give an idea of the maximum number of sales that could be expected. Secondly, firms can pay to have a sample survey conducted. This is where a small number of people who are representative of consumers likely to buy the product are asked questions relevant to the **launch** of a new product. The publishing firm, for instance, might ask what stories would be of interest, how much would be paid for a magazine of this sort, and how frequently the magazine might be purchased. Some products will then be given a test launch. A small group of consumers may be given the product to try out and then are asked questions about it. Or the product may be put on sale in one region of the UK to see how it sells before the firm spends money equipping a factory to produce it for the whole of the UK and for export.

Exercise

Describe the product or products sold by one company which has premises in your locality. Have they launched any new products recently? If so, what, and how did the company attempt to market that product?

Location

Having decided what to sell, a firm must decide where to locate its business premises. A number of factors will influence its decision:

- The location of the market for a product. In some industries, such as retailing, it is essential to be near to consumers who will buy the product. It would be foolish for a large department store to be situated at Land's End! In other industries, the cost of transporting the finished product may be very high in proportion to its value, so local firms selling in local markets have a big cost advantage over those who transport products over long distances.

- The location of raw materials. A coal mine can only be located on top of or very near coal. A British steel plant needs to be located near ports where iron ore can be shipped in cheaply from abroad.

- The availability of suitable labour. It is essential that a firm is able to recruit suitable labour. The cost of labour as well as the cost of training or retraining are important considerations.

- Site costs. The costs of buying or renting land and premises are another important factor affecting location. The government may give financial help to firms setting up in areas of very high unemployment.

- The local infrastructure and economic environment of a region. A firm's overall costs may be reduced if, for instance, it is located near a motorway or a port, or if there are many suppliers of components already in an area, or if local colleges and universities provide courses and expertise of direct relevance to the industry.

- Historical factors. A firm with an existing factory is likely to make use of these facilities rather than set up a new plant when it wants to launch a new product. The cost of moving is very high—firms rarely move to new locations, once they are established in a particular area.

Exercise

Describe where the company you chose in the previous exercise is located. Why is it located in that particular place rather than elsewhere in the locality or elsewhere in Britain?

Finance

Launching a new product or a new business is likely to be a costly affair. There are several ways in which money can be raised to pay for new *investment*. One way is for a firm to borrow money. It may do this from an ordinary high street bank—like Barclay's or Lloyd's—or from an industrial bank which specializes in lending money to companies. For a very small company, members of the family, or friends, may be prepared to lend it money.

Another way to raise money is to sell new **shares** in the firm. In return for buying these shares, the new shareholders will expect to be paid a share of the profits that the business makes. Very big companies are likely to be quoted on the London Stock Exchange and can sell new shares on the London money markets. Smaller companies may sell shares in local markets—stock exchanges exist in Birmingham and Manchester, for example. Or, as with loans, banks, particularly industrial banks, or friends and relatives may be willing to invest in a company by buying new shares.

The government may be willing to contribute towards new investment if a company intends to create jobs in an area of very high unemployment or in any industry eligible for special assistance. The government also runs various schemes to allow small businesses to borrow at lower interest rates from banks or claim extra tax relief for shareholders.

But by far the most important source of investment money— between 50 and 70% of all such funds—comes from companies themselves. Instead of giving all the profit that they make over a year to shareholders, businesses **retain** part of the **profit** for investment purposes. Shareholders do not necessarily lose out because of this: they might have a lower profit share in one year, but should see the value of the shareholding grow as the firm grows through investment.

Exercise

Look through a past copy or copies of quality newspapers (the *Financial Times* would be the best). Find an advertisement or a story which gives details of a firm raising money for investment. Write a short report about it.

Production

With a product to sell and money to finance the business, a firm now has to face the problems of production. In order to produce, it is likely to need what economists call **factors of production**—

Source:
The Stock
Exchange

land, labour and capital. Land includes not only that on which to build business premises but also all the raw materials which the earth produces—everything from fish to uranium. A business will certainly need workers, such as production line workers, managers, sales people and office staff. It will also need capital—machines and buildings to allow production to take place. It will be the job of management to combine these factors of production in order to ensure the right level of production at least cost.

Exercise

Describe how the product of the local company you have chosen in the exercise on 'Product' is produced. How are the factors of production combined in the production process?

103

Sales

Once the product is in production, a firm has to sell it. It may produce to order—like a shipyard building a new destroyer for the Royal Navy or a hairdresser cutting somebody's hair. Or goods may be produced in anticipation of sales being made—like toys to be sold in the shops at Christmas. Some firms don't need to worry about sales: orders come in without the firm needing to do anything. But these firms are very rare indeed. Most firms devote part of their resources to securing sales. They do this by employing sales staff who meet customers personally or speak to them on the telephone. A business may advertise in specialist magazines, in local and national newspapers, on television, on bill boards, to name but a few outlets. Other forms of **promotion** include special packaging of products, displays at exhibitions and trade fairs, mail shots and brochures. This all costs money. For instance, about one-quarter of the price of a typical branded box of washing powder represents the cost of advertising and other promotions needed to sell it to the consumer.

Exercise

Describe how the local company you have already written about tries to sell its products. Write particularly about advertising or other promotional campaigns undertaken.

Profits

All private businesses need to be aware of their finances. The most important figure is the **profit** or **loss** figure, because if the firm makes losses over a long period it is likely to go bankrupt. If it fails to make good profits, the shareholders of the company may become dissatisfied and sell their shares or attempt to have the management replaced.

Profit is the difference between total revenue and total cost. **Total revenue** is the sum of all the monies received by the firm. For most companies, the largest source of revenue is from the sale of the products that they produce. For instance, a company manufacturing cookers may sell 10 000 a year at an average price of £300: its total revenue from sales would then be 10 000 × £300, or £3 million. Revenue may also be derived from sources such as interest on money the company has saved, royalties on products produced under licence by other companies, and rent on buildings and premises hired out.

Total cost is the sum of all monies paid out by the firm. Examples of costs are wages paid to workers, monies paid for raw materials, rates paid to the local authority and interest paid on loans made by the business. Some costs are known as **fixed costs** or **overhead costs**. These are costs which a business has to pay whether or not it produces anything. For instance, for a local corner shop, the cost of the premises is a fixed cost because rents, rates, repairs and maintenance or repayments on a mortgage have to be paid whether or not a single item is sold in any week. **Variable costs** are those which vary with output: the more that is produced, the higher will be the total variable cost. Examples of variable costs for a record company would be the raw materials to make each record, such as plastic and electricity.

The sales point where total cost just equals total revenue is known as the **break-even point**. It's the point where the company isn't making a loss but neither is it making a profit. Extra sales should push the company into profitability; fewer sales will result in losses.

Profits of the company are used for three purposes. Firstly, the business may well have to pay taxes to the government on its profit. Secondly, it is likely to retain part of the profit to plough back into the business for investment. Thirdly, shareholders of the company will receive a **dividend**—a share of the profits.

Exercise

Make a list of the likely fixed costs for the local company you have chosen in the exercises above and the likely variable costs.

A successful company

What is a successful company? There is no simple answer to this question because it will depend upon whose point of view is being considered. For instance, from a worker's point of view, a successful company will be one which pays high wages and offers good conditions of service. But from a purely business point of view, a successful company is one which makes high profits. In order to generate high profits, the company will have to produce goods as efficiently as possible, which includes producing them at the lowest cost possible. The quality of a product will have to be right as well as its design. The company will be marketing its product successfully and pricing it at a level which will give maximum profits in the long run. Sales should expand. Relations with workers in the company, with suppliers and with customers should be good. Research, development and investment should be high on the list of priorities for this firm.

Every market economy needs its firms to be successful if **living standards** are to continue to rise. A major problem faced by the UK, certainly over the past 40 years and probably for much longer than that, is that British industry has not been particularly successful in comparison with industries in other countries. The result has been lower growth in living standards and more unemployment than need have been the case. So successful firms are vital for Britain now and in the future.

Exercise

Why is the success of the local company you have written about in previous exercises in this chapter important for the local economy?

Important points to keep in mind

1. A prime function of a business is to produce goods and services.
2. A firm has to decide what it will sell, where it will sell it and what price to charge for it.
3. Production processes ideally should be as efficient as possible—products should be produced at lowest cost in the right location.
4. Firms need money to finance their development. The cost of research and development and investment comes from sources such as retained profits, loans and the issuing of new share capital.
5. Firms are in business to make profits. Profit is the difference between revenue and costs. Profits are used to pay taxes and to reinvest in the firm and to reward shareholders for risking their capital in the company.

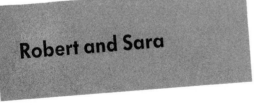

Robert and Sara

Robert Mitchell and Sara Penn are unemployed. They've talked for some time about setting up their own business, but they haven't got much money or many qualifications. A neighbour suggested that they might enter the window cleaning trade—no qualifications and little start-up money needed there. Robert and Sara decided to undertake a feasibility study for the business.

Location

Robert and Sara have to decide which area of their city to work in. They live in the All Souls district of Brumham. A westward cross-section of the city is shown on the map. Details of each area (called a 'ward') are shown in the accompanying statistical table.

106

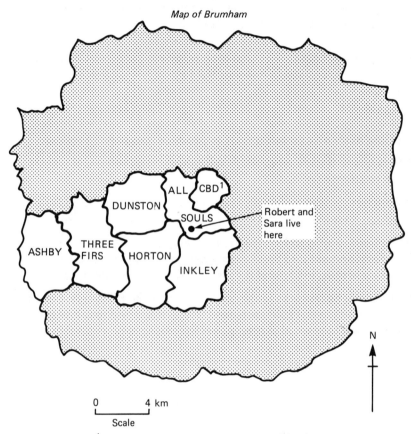

Map of Brumham

ALL CBD[1]

DUNSTON

SOULS

Robert and Sara live here

THREE FIRS

ASHBY

HORTON

INKLEY

N

0   4 km

Scale

[1] Central Business District — the centre of the city

Wards of Brumham: *Selected statistics*

Area	Total number of dwellings	Housing tenure			Type of houses			Car ownership				Percentage unemployment
		Owner occupied	*Council housing*	*Other*	*Flats*	*Houses*	*Other*	*No car*	*1 car*	*2 cars*	*3 cars*	
Dunston	3403	1114	1842	402	478	2788	137	2429	871	93	10	28.2
Three Firs	2986	2562	192	232	121	2845	20	1090	1482	372	42	8.2
Ashby	3545	2719	316	510	456	3043	46	641	1572	1108	224	5.1
Horton	2606	1377	477	752	293	1935	378	1635	833	116	22	25.4
Inkley	2654	767	1442	445	300	2336	15	1846	74	84	10	25.0
All Souls	3559	74	3266	219	2650	871	38	2871	635	45	8	28.7

TASK 1

What factors should Robert and Sara take into account when making their decision about where to work? Make a list of points which you think are important.

TASK 2

If the area you have chosen already has a firm which offers window cleaning services, would your decision be any different? Write a 100-word report on this.

TASK 3

Look carefully at the map and the statistics accompanying it. Robert and Sara will only have time to cover one of the six areas shown. Which area do you think this should be? Write a 200-word report justifying your decision. You may assume that Robert and Sara have a car and that none of the six districts has a window cleaning service offered already.

1 Ward in which Robert and Sara work	2 Number of kilometres travelled per year	3 Hours of normal work per year	4 Travelling time per year	5 Hours available to clean houses per year	6 Number of houses that could be cleaned in a year	7 Number of customer households needed if each house-hold is cleaned ten times a year
All Souls	2000		100			
Inkley	4000		200			
Dunston	4000		200			
Horton	4000		200			
Three Firs	6000		300			
Ashby	8000		400			

Time and distance

TASK

1 They decide that a 'normal working year would be 8 hours' work per day, 5 days a week, 45 weeks a year. How many hours' work a year will they work on this basis? Record your answer in Column 3. It will, of course, be the same in all wards.

2 Part of their time will be spent travelling to and from the area in which they decide to work. Calculate the number of hours left to clean houses in a year. Record your answer in Column 5.

3 Robert and Sara estimate they they can clean one house's windows in 20 minutes, working together. In Column 6, record the number of houses that Robert and Sara could clean in one year, assuming that they worked their 'normal' working year.

4 To provide a regular service, they estimate that each customer could want his or her windows cleaned ten times a year. How many households would Robert and Sara need to have as customers if they were to work their normal working year? Record your answer in Column 7.

108

Launching the service

Here are some ideas that Robert and Sara could use to find customers.

◆ Put advertisements in the local free newspaper. The cost for a 24-word advert for one day is £5.00.

◆ Print a simple leaflet and distribute it to every household in the chosen district. The cost per thousand leaflets would be £50.

◆ Put advertisements in local shop windows—cost 20p per week per shop.

◆ Go round each house in the area and ask whether or not they wish to make use of the service offered.

TASK 1

Are there any other ways in which Robert and Sara could attract new customers? If so, what?

TASK 2

Write a 100-word report explaining how you think Robert and Sara should launch their window cleaning service and why they should do it in this way.

Costs

Robert and Sara face the following costs:

Car

Purchase of second-hand car	£250
Car insurance	£100
Car tax (12 months)	£120
Running costs of car (petrol, repairs, servicing etc.)*	15p per km

Other equipment

Ladders (second-hand)	£30
Buckets	£16
Leathers and sponges	£8

Notional wages per person

Yearly wage for all work up to a **maximum** of 8 hours per day, 5 days a week, 45 weeks a year, i.e. 1800 hours work per year	£3600
Overtime, per hour, per worker	£2

Interest

Interest on a loan taken out for 12 months to pay for the equipment	£76

* The table 'Time and Distance' gives the number of kilometres Robert and Sara would have to travel yearly to and from the area in which they work. In addition, they will need to move around the area to clean houses. Assume that they have to travel an extra 150 kilometres for every 1000 houses they clean (i.e. it will cost an extra £15 in travel costs for every 1000 houses cleaned on top of the fixed cost of travel to and from work).

TASK 1

Which of these are fixed costs (i.e. costs which do **not** change with the number of houses cleaned) and which are variable costs (i.e. costs which **do** increase the more houses are cleaned)? Calculate the total value of fixed costs for the ward of the city in which you have chosen to work. In order to calculate the yearly running cost of the car, consult the table on 'Time and Distance'. Don't forget that both Robert and Sara need to be paid a wage.

TASK 2

Now complete the following table of costs:

Number of houses cleaned per year	Total fixed cost (£)	Total variable cost (£)	Total costs (fixed plus variable cost)
1000			
2000			
3000			
4500			
6000			
7500			
15000			
25000			

TASK 3

Robert and Sara could buy a handcart to carry their equipment instead of a car. The handcart would only cost £20 to buy. But, it would mean that they could only clean houses in the All Souls, Inkley and Horton wards of the city. It would also increase travelling time to 2 hours per 8-hour day. Should they buy the handcart?

Market research and revenue

Robert and Sara didn't know how much to charge, or how many households would want to use their window cleaning service. So they decided to conduct some market research. They selected six roads on the edge of their chosen area each with about 50 houses. Each road contained a similar mix of housing and was typical of the housing in the ward. Robert and Sara called at each house in each road asking whether or not the occupants wanted their windows cleaned, on a regular basis (ten times a year). Each road was quoted a different price. Here is the response that Robert and Sara got.

Price quoted (£)	% households wanting their windows cleaned
1.00	60
1.50	30
2.00	15
2.50	6
3.00	4

TASK 1

Calculate the number of households that would want their windows to be cleaned in the ward of the city you have decided to work in at each price. Then calculate the total number of houses to be cleaned in a year given that each household will have its windows cleaned ten times a year. Assume that the results of the market research provide an accurate picture of demand for window cleaning services in your chosen ward. Record your calculation on the following table.

Price charged (£)	Number of households wanting windows cleaned in your ward*	Total number of houses cleaned in one year assuming each house is cleaned ten times a year
1.00		
1.50		
2.00		
2.50		
3.00		

* Round up or down to a whole number any fractions resulting from your calculation.

110

TASK 2

Draw up a demand schedule for the whole of the ward in which Robert and Sara have chosen to work, showing the relationship between the price charged and quantity demanded (in this case, the quantity demanded is the number of houses cleaned in a year). Plot the graph using the following axes:

Price

Number of houses cleaned per year

TASK 3

Calculate the total 'revenue' or 'turnover' generated at different levels of price. To calculate total revenue or turnover, multiply the price charged per house cleaned by the number of houses cleaned in a year:

Price (£)	Number of houses cleaned per year	Total revenue (£)
1.00		
1.50		
2.00		
2.50		
3.00		

TASK 4

Draw a total revenue schedule. Do this by plotting total revenue against the number of households demanding a window clean. Use the following graph:

Total revenue (£)

Number of houses cleaned per year

Prices and output

How many houses should Robert and Sara clean? How many houses do they need to clean in order just to break even? How much should they charge for their services?

TASK 1

To help you answer these questions, draw a graph combining your findings on costs and prices. On the graph below, copy out the previous total cost schedule and total revenue schedule.

Total
revenue
total
cost (£)

Number of houses cleaned per year

Now state:

- Between what levels of output would Robert and Sara make a loss on their business?
- At what level of output would they just break even?
- Between what levels of output would Robert and Sara make a profit?

TASK 2

Now decide how many houses Robert and Sara should clean each year. When making your decision, remember that:

- profit earned in the business is the difference between total revenue and total cost
- in winter, there are only about 8 daylight hours per day; if they want to give a regular service to customers, they cannot take on much more work than this throughout the year.

Having decided how many houses should be cleaned each year, use the demand schedule to fix a price for each 'clean'.

The window cleaning business has been going now for two years. Robert and Sara have been worried about their car: it keeps breaking down, involving costly repairs and lost revenue, because they then can't get to their district to clean windows. Over the past 12 months, the car has broken down 6 times, resulting in:

- 12 lost working days
- £250 repair costs

A 'new' second-hand car would cost £550 and they would get £50 in part-exchange for their old one.

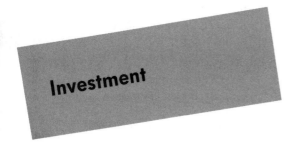

Investment

TASK 1

What factors should Robert and Sara take into consideration when deciding whether or not to replace their car?

TASK 2

Assuming that Robert and Sara would have to borrow the money to buy their new car, should they buy it? To help your decision, complete the following table which shows a number of different possible future situations. Assume that the average cost of each repair is £50, and that two working days are lost per breakdown while the car is being repaired.

		Keeping old car Lost revenue from not being able to work due to break-downs	*Cost of repairs*	*Total cost*	*Buying new car* Lost revenue from not being able to work due to break-downs	*Cost of repairs*	*Purchase cost of new car*	*Total cost*
Case	*Assumptions*							
1	Old car breaks down 12 times in a year—new car trouble-free							
2	Old car breaks down 6 times in a year—new car breaks down 3 times							
3	Old car breaks down 6 times in a year—new car breaks down 6 times too							

Taking on an extra employee

Two years on and Robert and Sara are doing well with their business. They are now considering whether or not to take on an extra worker (or, as it is put in economics, a 'marginal' worker). An extra worker would cost £1.50 per hour. Robert and Sara would also have to pay employers' national insurance contributions to the government, at a rate of 5% of the employee's wages.

They think that by taking on an extra worker, they will be able to clean another 2250 houses per year at a price of £2.00 per house.

TASK 1

Calculate the extra cost (or the 'marginal' cost) of taking on an extra worker. Then calculate the extra revenue (or the 'marginal' revenue) gained by employing that worker. Will they make more profit as a result?

TASK 2

Now work out whether or not the extra worker will be profitable if:

- he or she were employed at £2 an hour

- he or she were employed at £2.50 an hour

- he or she were employed at £2 an hour but the government made the worker exempt from all national insurance contributions

- he or she were on a Youth Training Scheme placement with Robert and Sara (the cost of the worker to them would be zero).

11 The government

The public sector in the UK is responsible for spending over 40% of all the income generated in the economy in a year and is made up of three parts. Firstly, there is central government, controlled from the Houses of Parliament at Westminster. Secondly, there is local government. Each area in the UK has a local authority which is responsible for providing services at a local level as well as passing local laws. Examples of local authorities are Kent or Staffordshire or Dyfed. Thirdly, there are a large number of government bodies, independent but answerable to either local or central government. Examples are organizations such as the BBC, British Rail and the Severn–Trent Water Authority.

Public spending

One of the most important functions of government is to provide goods and services for citizens of the UK. Look at the table of public expenditure by programme for 1984/5. The most expensive programme was Social Security—spending on benefits such as the state retirement pension, unemployment benefit, supplementary benefit and child benefit. Defence was the next most expensive programme—spending on the armed forces at home and abroad. Then came the National Health Service, costing an estimated £15.8 billion. All of these programmes are provided mainly by central government. The most important local authority programme is education, costing an estimated £13.7 billion in 1984/5. Other programmes which are provided mainly by local authorities are housing, arts and libraries and 'other environmental services' (which would include refuse collection and provision of public parks).

There are a number of reasons why so much of the nation's money is spent by government. Firstly, some goods and services would not be provided if they were not provided by governments. Take street lighting, for instance. Imagine a situation where the local authority did not provide any street lighting. How many people would buy and maintain, say, a street light outside their house? Who would buy street lights for the main roads? Yet without street lights, there would be more crime on Britain's streets, more car accidents and anybody wanting to walk out at night would be severely inconvenienced. So because the provision of street lighting would be totally inadequate if left in private hands,

Table 1 *Public expenditure by programme*
          (cash terms)

	£billion 1984–85 estimated outturn
Defence	17.2
Overseas aid and other overseas services	2.5
Agriculture, fisheries, food and forestry	2.1
Industry, energy, trade and employment	7.2
Arts and libraries	0.7
Transport	4.8
Housing	3.1
Other environmental services	3.8
Law, order and protective services	5.1
Education and science	13.7
Health and personal social services	15.8
Social security	37.9
Other	14.2
Planning total	**128.1**

Source: The Treasury, *Economic Progress Report*, January 1985

government steps in, provides street lights and charges everybody in the area a small amount to cover the cost. This type of good is known as a 'public good'. Other examples are the judiciary, lighthouses and the armed forces. (Imagine a country defended by private armies! Would you pay for a private army?)

For some goods, private provision could well lead to under-consumption. Imagine a situation where there were no state schools and colleges; everybody had to pay for education. What would happen is that at least some parents would either not send their children to school or those children would not stay on at school or college for as long a period as they would do if education were free. Education benefits the individual not only because it improves his or her chances of getting a good job, but also because an educated person will be able to participate more fully in the society of which he or she forms a part. It also benefits the community. Without a well-educated population, the UK would not compete successfully with other economies around the world and would fail to share in their increasing prosperity. Less educated workers would also need more support. As low paid or unemployed, they and their families would receive a wide range of benefits which the better off in society would have to pay for. So, it makes sense to encourage people to stay in the education system for as long as it will benefit them and an effective way of doing that is by providing free state education.

A third reason for state provision of goods is that collective provision is often the most efficient. Economic efficiency has a number of different aspects but they include cost, quality, choice and equality. If the state can produce goods at lower cost, sell them at a lower price, produce better quality and more advanced goods, give a greater range of goods for consumers to choose from and distribute these more fairly than the private sector, then public provision of goods is obviously desirable.

In practice, it is not always easy to see whether or not the state is a more efficient provider of goods and services than the private sector. Take the National Health Service, which is very cost effective. The UK spends a lower proportion of its income on health than countries such as France, Germany and the USA where health care is mostly provided by the private sector. It's certainly a fair system—treatment is given not on the basis of whether or not you can afford it, but whether or not you are ill; it is also a very high quality service. But, private health care is growing in popularity in Britain, with schemes like BUPA growing in numbers each year. This is because private health care provides more choice, and can often provide a quicker service and better facilities. So the NHS is more efficient in some ways than private health care, but in other ways it is less so. Economists can only point out these differences: it's up to the ordinary person in the street to decide whether or not he or she wants the state to provide free health care for all or have some different system relying on private provision.

A fourth reason for public expenditure is to ensure a fair distribution of income in an economy. If the government only provided public goods (items such as defence and the judiciary), and left everything else to the private sector, then without a doubt people would die of starvation, cold and poor health in today's Britain. It would be the unemployed, the very young, the old, people who had long-term illnesses or were physically or mentally handicapped, who would be most vulnerable. How much these sort of people should be helped is a matter of great debate because normally the more the state gives to the poor, the more it has to take away from the rich. When you become a worker and start paying taxes, you may well feel that you are losing too much money to the state to pay for benefits for others. On the other hand, if you retire or have a serious accident at work which leaves you disabled for the rest of your life, you may well feel that the state gives you too little.

Lastly, public expenditure can be used with taxes to influence the workings of the economy as a whole and its constituent parts. This will be considered in further detail later on in the chapter.

Exercise

Make a list of all the property owned by public sector bodies in your locality. If possible, locate them on a map. Briefly describe the services offered by each location.

Taxation

Public spending has to be paid for, and the main source is tax receipts. As can be seen from the table of government receipts, the biggest single tax collected in the UK is personal (income) tax, a tax on income earned over a year by an individual. Other important taxes are Value Added Tax, a 15% tax on most goods and services; excise duties, a tax mainly on alcohol, tobacco and petrol; rates, a local authority tax on property; and petroleum revenue tax, a tax on North Sea oil.

Table 2 Government receipts

	1985–86 forecast £billion
General government taxation	
Income tax	35.2
Value-added tax	18.3
Local authority rates	13.6
Corporation tax	10.1
Oil duties	6.5
Petroleum revenue tax	8.2
Spirits, beer, wine, cider and perry duties	4.2
Tobacco duties	4.3
Vehicle excise duty	2.5
Taxes on capital	1.9
European Community duties	1.5
Other (including accruals adjustment)	4.6
Total	**110.9**
North Sea oil royalties, etc.	2.5
National insurance, etc. contributions	24.6
Gross trading surplus and rent	3.0
Interest and dividend receipts	6.4
Other	2.7
Total general government receipts	150.1
General government borrowing requirement	9.4
Total general government receipts and borrowing	**159.5**

Source: The Treasury, *Economic Progress Report*, March/April 1985

Taxes are used not only to raise revenue for the government but also to influence the economy. Why the government should wish to influence the economy and how it might do so is the subject of the rest of this chapter.

Exercise

What taxes do you pay now? What taxes will you pay when you become a worker?

The government is responsible for promoting the well-being of its citizens, a very important part of which is economic well-being. Since the Second World War, British governments have attempted to use government power to bring about

- as low an unemployment rate as possible

- as low an inflation rate as possible

- a situation where Britain pays her way in the world by exporting at least as much as she imports

- a growth in living standards for the population as a whole

- a just distribution of income and wealth between citizens.

They have rarely if ever succeeded in achieving all of these objectives, but that doesn't mean that governments haven't tried in the past or shouldn't try in the future. One of the reasons for failure has been that economists and politicians don't really know how the economy works. There is no shortage of theories or ideas about such important questions as 'how can unemployment be reduced?' or 'what causes inflation?', but nobody has come up with a theory which everybody agrees with and which has been shown to be definitely correct.

The government can influence the economy in two main ways, firstly through government spending and taxation and, secondly, through laws and regulations.

Taking the first way, some economists believe that more government spending or lower taxes will lead to more jobs and a better standard of living for the country as a whole. If the government spends more money, or citizens spend more money because they have to pay lower taxes, that money will have to be spent on goods and services. That spending directly benefits citizens and reduces unemployment because somebody has to produce the extra goods and services being demanded. Other economists, however, believe that this policy leads to inflation, more imports and a loss of competitiveness of British industry. In the long term, unemployment will rise as the economy loses ground against international competitors.

Government spending and taxation has also been used to try and affect the allocation of resources in the economy. Some economists argue that government subsidies and taxes have a powerful impact on the decisions of businesses, consumers and workers. For instance, raising taxes on profits is likely to make some business people work less hard to earn profits for their companies; investment plans may be shelved as the project ceases to be profitable enough; British money may flow abroad to be invested in lower-taxed foreign companies. Raising income tax may lead to workers working less hard; they may be less willing to accept promotion or work overtime at the higher tax rates. Raising taxes on goods and services, such as a rise in excise duty on tobacco, will reduce the amount bought. In the case of tobacco, that's good news for the country's health but bad news for tobacco companies and their workers. Subsidizing (i.e. paying money to) railways will encourage more people to use them and will help keep the environment clean. It will hit the car industry though, and the money could perhaps have been better spent on subsidizing a high technology industry of the future which would in the long run contribute more jobs and more income to the economy than the increased public money spent on the railways.

Economists differ in their analysis of what the exact effects of a change in taxes on public spending will be. Some argue that Britain's poor performance as an economy over the past 30 years has been due to the fact that too much government spending has meant high taxes. These high taxes have discouraged workers from earning money and business from making high profits. The money the government spent would have been far better left in the hands of the taxpayer to spend as he or she wanted. Other economists argue that Britain has not had particularly high government spending over the past 30 years and, anyway, taxes have little effect on a firm's or worker's desire to make more money.

Exercise

What would be the economic effects on different parts of the economic community of (a) a rise in the rate of VAT on food from 0% to 15% and (b) a 20% cut in supplementary benefit rates?

Laws and regulations

The government also intervenes in the economy through laws and regulations. Every part of economic activity is controlled, from the way in which a worker is paid to how much pollution a factory can be allowed to create; from where a business can site itself to whom a company must sell to; and so on. The purpose of all these laws and regulations is to protect other economic agents from the activity of one company, consumer, etc. For instance, if a company wanted to build a factory handling dangerous chemicals at the bottom of your garden, it is obvious that that would affect your economic welfare. Similarly, if your local super-market can only sell your favourite brand of baked beans at a very high price fixed by the manufacturer, then you will be affected.

Regulations, though, may have bad effects. For instance, it is often claimed that workers today have so many rights that businesses are reluctant to take on full-time workers. If the firm handling dangerous chemicals is not allowed to set up at the bottom of your garden, then it might shelve its investment plan altogether or set up a plant abroad, resulting in fewer British jobs and a loss of income.

Is government good for Britain? Some government must be good. In a sophisticated modern economy, government is essential for its smooth running. How it should work, though, is more difficult to say. There is no easy answer. Each government must be judged separately on its own merits.

Important points to keep in mind

☐1 **Government is made up of three parts—central government, local government and other bodies such as British Rail.**

☐2 **Government spends about 40% of all that is produced in Britain on programmes such as defence, education and health.**

☐3 **Government finances most of this spending by raising taxes.**

☐4 **Government, through its policies, can influence every individual in society. It can affect them, for instance, by influencing the level of unemployment, the rate of inflation, the level of imports and exports, the growth of incomes in the economy and the distribution of incomes in an economy.**

Spending

Source: The Treasury, *Economic Progress Report* No. 174, January 1985

Planned public spending for 1985–86: where, who and what

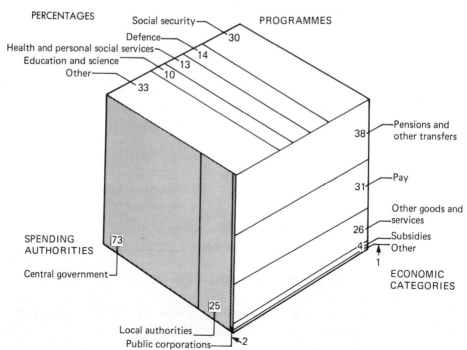

PERCENTAGES   PROGRAMMES

Social security — 30
Defence — 14
Health and personal social services — 13
Education and science — 10
Other — 33

38 — Pensions and other transfers

31 — Pay

26 — Other goods and services

4 — Subsidies
3 — Other
1

SPENDING AUTHORITIES   73
Central government —

25
Local authorities
Public corporations — 2

ECONOMIC CATEGORIES

TASK

1. What percentage of total government spending in 1985/6 was it planned to spend on: (*a*) defence; (*b*) public sector pay; (*c*) social security; (*d*) local authorities; (*e*) pensions and other transfers?

2. Planned public expenditure in 1985/6 was £132 billion (a billion is a thousand million). What was the planned expenditure in £billion on each of the five items listed in question 1?

3. A government wishes to make large cuts in public spending. Why would the social security programme be an obvious target? Which economic category would be reduced by large cuts in the social security programme?

4. If the government increased spending on its defence programme by half, by recruiting more men, and half by spending on equipment, which 'economic categories' and which 'spending authorities' would be affected?

5. Which public spending programmes are the direct responsibility of local authorities?

Privatization

Complaints over privatised school cleaning

121

Wendy Berliner
Education Correspondent

A private firm hired to clean schools in the London borough of Merton has been given two weeks to improve its standards or it could face the sack by the local authority. This follows an avalanche of complaints about the dirty state of many schools in the borough since term started on Tuesday. Some heads have already warned parents that they intend to send children home if the situation does not improve.

The firm, Academy Cleaning, took over cleaning functions from council employees at the end of the summer term, after action was taken by the Conservative-controlled authority to save money by privatising school cleaning and meals.

Many schools have reportedly not had their annual thorough summer cleaning, normally carried out when schools are empty. Some head teachers have closed parts of schools, which are considered too dirty to use.

There have been reports of a home economics room out of use because of grime-encrusted window sills and uncleaned bird droppings, and a craft room where shavings and debris from the end of the summer term have not been cleared up. Showers in another school are reported out of use because they have not been cleaned.

In other cases there are said to be signs that haste has led to improper cleaning, with dirt being polished into desks and cleaning agents inadequately cleaned off surfaces.

Schools of about 1,000 pupils, which used to have a squad of about a dozen women arriving at the end of the day to clear up, are alleged to have been assigned only two people.

Some cleaners have been turning up late at night, and in one instance they set off a burglar alarm and the police were called. In another instance cleaners turned up at 10 pm and a caretaker refused to let them in.

Source: The Guardian, September 1983

TASK

1. What is meant by a 'private firm'?

2. Who used to clean Merton's schools before Academy Cleaning?

3. What complaints were made about the standard of cleaning by Academy Cleaning?

4. Why did Merton Borough Council privatize school cleaning services?

5. To what extent is the new privatized cleaning service more efficient than the old council-provided service?

Tax changes

	Effect on government revenue in a full year (£million)
Income tax	
Change basic rate by 1p	1025
Change all higher rates by 1p	70
Change single and wife's earned income allowance by £100	380
Change married man's allowance by £100	320
Indirect taxes	
Change VAT by 1%	1200
Change beer by 1p/pint	95
Change wine by 10p/bottle	50
Change spirits by £1/bottle	100
Change tobacco duty by equivalent of 5p on packet of 20 king size cigarettes	175
Change petrol by 10p/gallon	500
Change vehicle excise duty (car licence) by £10	180

Source: The Treasury, *Economic Progress Report Supplement,* December 1983

TASK

1 Calculate the effect on government revenue if:

   a the basic rate of income tax were raised by 2p in the pound

   b the married man's allowance were increased by £300

   c the tax on wine were reduced by 5p a bottle and

   d the licence for a car were raised by £30

2 The government decided to increase the tax on tobacco by the equivalent of 50p on a packet of 20 king sized cigarettes. What would be the possible effects of this on: (*a*) smokers; (*b*) government revenues; (*c*) taxpayers who smoke; (*d*) taxpayers who don't smoke; (*e*) the health service; (*f*) workers in the tobacco industry; (*g*) workers in other industries in the economy; (*h*) imports into Britain? If the money raised were used to spend more on the health service, would the government be right or wrong to implement this change? Reason your argument carefully.

3 The government wants to reduce taxes by £2000 million. Which tax or taxes should it reduce? Why should it do this? Explain your answer with reference to the effects on jobs, inflation, living standards, exports and imports, and any other relevant factors.

Rates

123

South Staffordshire District Council spending by programme

Programme	Gross Expend-iture £000
Planning	634
Leisure	771
Health	713
Refuse	762
Housing	825
Other	1,401
	5,106

Housing Revenue

Fees, charges and miscellaneous income	101	0.9
Interest on mortgages	635	5.4
Rents	5,078	43.2
Interest on balances	700	6.0
Use of balances	123	1.0
	6,637	56.5
	11,743	100.0

South Staffordshire District Council Budget 1985–86

What the council spends its money on

124

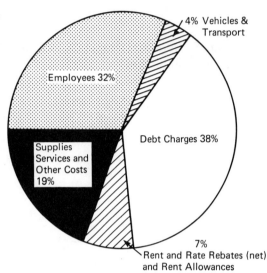

- 4% Vehicles & Transport
- Employees 32%
- Debt Charges 38%
- Supplies Services and Other Costs 19%
- 7% Rent and Rate Rebates (net) and Rent Allowances

How many people are employed?[1]

Rate Fund:	1985/86
Planning	35.6
Leisure	40.5
Health	28.0
Refuse	49.5
Housing	2.0
Other	23.0
Housing Revenue	42.0
Central Establishment[2]	94.1
Works[3]	101.0
	415.7

Notes
1 Figures include full time equivalents for part time staff and are based on the budgets.
2 Central establishment covers all central services such as finance, administration, legal, architectural etc, the costs of which are charged out to service users.
3 Works covers the Council's housing repairs, green areas and sewerage teams whose costs are charged out to service users.

TASK

1. What are 'rates'?

2. Name the five largest spending programmes for South Staffordshire District Council.

3. Which of these spending programmes had (a) the largest and (b) the smallest net expenditure?

4. How does the Council raise money on housing in South Staffordshire apart from the rates?

5. What proportion of Council spending went on (a) employees and (b) debt charges?

6. How many people were employed in planning and leisure together in 1985/6?

7. What has happened to the amount the government has been giving to the Council to help pay for services over the period 1979 to 1986?

8. The Council decides to spend an extra £250 000 on extra leisure services in the district.

   a If it paid for this on the rates, what would have to be the approximate increase in the penny rate?
   b Who would have to pay these extra rates?
   c Where might jobs be gained and lost in the economy as a result?
   d Who would benefit and who would lose as a result of this increase in spending?

9. The government in 1986/7 decides to cut back its block grant to South Staffordshire District Council by a further £300 000. What services should the Council cut and why? What will be the effects of these cuts on jobs, the quality of local services and taxpayers?

125

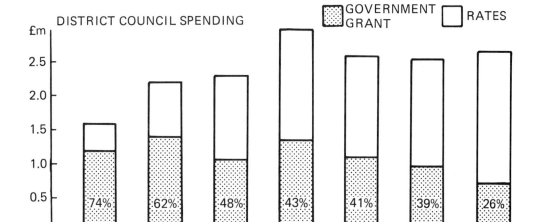

DISTRICT COUNCIL SPENDING — GOVERNMENT GRANT — RATES

£m
2.5
2.0
1.5
1.0
0.5

79/80 (74%) 80/81 (62%) 81/82 (48%) 82/83 (43%) 83/84 (41%) 84/85 (39%) 85/86 (26%)

YTS

TASK

1. What is the YTS?

2. Why does Youthaid suggest that in 1985 one-third of all places on the YTS remain unfilled?

3. According to Youthaid, how many YTS graduates on average:

   a get a real job after leaving the scheme
   b remain unemployed
   c go back to full-time education?

4. The YTS is paid for by government from taxpayers' money. Explain what effect you think YTS has on:

   a youth employment
   b the ability of youngsters to find a job
   c wages paid to young workers
   d the level of skills possessed by young workers

5. The article states that the government would have spent an extra £100 million on the YTS if all places on the scheme had been taken up. Explaining your answer carefully, do you think it would be best for this money to be used:

   a on helping unemployed YTS graduates to find jobs as suggested by the article
   b on giving bigger pensions to old-age pensioners
   c on giving income tax cuts
   d on providing extra monies for schools and colleges to expand provision for 17- and 18-year-olds?

Saving on YTS 'should be spent helping jobless'

The £100 million the Government will save because one in three places of the Youth Training Scheme remains unfilled, should be spent helping unemployed YTS graduates to find jobs, says Youthaid, an independent charity, in a report published today.

The low take-up of places is blamed partly on school leavers' disillusionment with the scheme.

Some 120,000 young people — more than a third — still cannot find a real job once they have completed their year on a YTS project. Those who drop out are just as likely to find a job as others who last the full course, says Youthaid.

The report shows that while just over half the YTS graduates do find jobs, a third remain unemployed across the country. A few keep their YTS jobs and some go back to school.

Locally, the unemployment rates for people who have completed YTS are in line with the rest of the population. In the North and Scotland 60 per cent of YTS graduates are out of work. This compares with 27 per cent of all 16–17 year olds who are unemployed nationally.

'One clear effect of the YTS is to reduce the wage expectations of school leavers and to make wages well below the average seem high compared to the allowance.'

The weekly allowance for people on the YTS is £26.25, compared with average weekly wages of £60 for 16–17 year olds.

Source: The Guardian, 4 February 1985

VAT

No VAT, Please, Chancellor

When the dreaded Value Added Tax was first imported into Britain, children's shoes were zero-rated because a Government report had concluded 'the price of children's footwear is an important factor in the context of foot abnormalities' and that 'there is a need to keep children's footwear as cheap as possible'.

Those conclusions still hold good, but now there's a rumour that the Chancellor might impose VAT on children's shoes in the next Budget. As if their shoes were not expensive enough already!

The price is prohibitive for some families. Chiropodist Steve Kennedy, who recently moved from Hastings to work for the Grimsby Health Authority, wrote to us: 'A major problem I have here in Immingham that I never had previously is "hand me down" shoes. This of course results in poor feet.'

High prices also deter parents from replacing outgrown shoes as often as they should. And shoes kept 'for best' may be brought into everyday use long after the child's feet have grown out of them.

But why do the prices have to be so high? Apparently we are paying for the choice, rather than just the shoe. For *each style of shoe*, a retailer would have to stock 80 boxes to carry the whole range of sizes and width fittings!

Source: Woman, 2 February 1985

TASK

1 What is Value Added Tax?

2 Children's shoes are 'zero-rated' for VAT purposes. What does this mean? What is the standard rate of VAT on goods and services?

3 Explain in your own words what conclusion the government report quoted in the passage came to.

4 Why can children's shoes be a very expensive item in a family's budget? How do some families cut down on this expense? What are the possible effects on their children's feet?

5 What effects might the imposition of VAT on children's shoes have on shoe sales and on children's feet?

6 The government is always presented with choices. Imagine you were Chancellor of the Exchequer and faced with three alternatives:

1 keep children's shoes zero-rated or
2 impose VAT on children's shoes and use the money to cut income tax by $\frac{1}{2}$p in the pound or
3 impose VAT on children's shoes and use the money to build and run a hospital with 200 beds

Which alternative do you think is the best? Explain the reasons for your decision carefully.

128

Wages Councils consultative paper

The Department of Employment has just issued a *Consultative Paper on Wages Councils*. It sets out options for the future of Wages Councils — should they be reformed or abolished?

Wages Councils, says the Paper, tend to reduce employment by fixing wages above the level at which people, especially the young, would be prepared to work. They make it illegal for employers to offer work at wages they can afford to pay and which the unemployed are prepared to accept. This applies in particular to jobs that could be offered by small employers.

Changed role

The wages levels set by the Wages Councils vary from £47.50 to £97.20 a week for full-time adults and from £29.71 to £59.20 for 16-year-olds. The 26 Wages Councils lay down minimum pay rates and detailed conditions for 2.75 million workers, primarily in the service industries. When they were first set up in 1909 they mostly covered manufacturing industries.

Two-thirds of the employees now covered by Wages Councils work only part-time and there are frequent complaints from employers that the Councils' awards are complex, lengthy and in many cases simply add to the red tape and bureaucracy of employing people; Wages Orders sometimes run to 30 pages in length and can be very difficult for both employers and employees to understand.

Many people argue that the only way to tackle these fundamental problems is to abolish the Wages Councils, saying that they serve only to harm job prospects for all the unemployed. Others say that the faults in the system could be dealt with by reform, that Councils could be limited to setting a single hourly rate, that their ability to award retrospective wage rises could be stopped, or that young people could be taken out of the system.

'On either view,' commented Employment Secretary Tom King, 'action is essential and urgent.'

Source: Department of Employment, *Employment News*, No. 129, March 1985

TASK

1. How many Wages Councils existed in March 1985?

2. What is the role of a Wages Council in an industry?

3. A Wages Council is a body appointed by the government which has the power to prosecute employers who fail to comply with its orders.

   a Why do you think a firm might try to avoid complying with a Wages Order?
   b What would be the effect on wages if Wages Councils were abolished?

4. Explain in your own words what the *Consultative Paper on Wages Councils* argues about the effect of Wages Councils on employment.

5. The article implies that there is a choice to be made between higher minimum wages and fewer jobs **or** lower wages and more jobs.

   a If this choice exists, which do you think is the better alternative?
   b Do you think that this choice exists at all? Is it not possible to have higher wages and more jobs?

   Explain both your answers carefully.

6. Do you think that it is the government's responsibility to prevent employers paying very low wages to workers? Give reasons for your decision.

12 The environment

130 **Man and his environment**

Every creature on this planet has an impact on the environment. Normally, these impacts are carefully balanced to provide a stable ecological framework. Occasionally the ecological balance will be disturbed and the natural environment will undergo a period of change until some new balance or equilibrium is found. This could involve the destruction of particular plants or minerals, or the disappearance of whole species.

Man is the animal which has had the most important single impact on the environment in the world's history. In a country like Britain, much of the face of the land has changed beyond recognition over the past 2000 years. Has this been a good thing or a bad thing? Economists can help answer the question by using the concept of social cost and social benefit.

Exercise

Find out about and write a short paragraph on the subject of 'ecology'. Why do man's economic activities disturb the ecological balance on our planet?

Private costs and benefits

Assume that you've just passed your driving test and that your parents have bought you a brand new car. What are the costs and benefits of that decision? So far as you are concerned, there are likely to be very few costs and many benefits. You might have to pay for petrol and part or all of the insurance, road tax and maintenance on the vehicle, although your parents are likely to help you out here. You will also spend time driving the car around which involves an opportunity cost to you because you could have been doing something else during that time like studying for your examinations, listening to a concert on radio or taking the dog for a walk. These costs are known as your 'private costs' because they are the costs borne by you as an individual economic agent. Your private benefits are likely to be numerous. You will have the freedom to travel the roads and get to places quickly and comfortably. A whole range of activities which were unavailable to you, or which were only available if your parents acted as taxi drivers, now become available. However, just because the private benefits of your having a car exceed the private costs, it does not necessarily follow that it is desirable that every young person should be a given a car.

Exercise

What would be the private costs and benefits to you if your parents paid for you to go on holiday by aeroplane to the Bahamas?

Social costs and benefits

The private costs and benefits of car ownership for you differ greatly from the costs and benefits to society of your owning a car—what are called by economists the 'social costs' and 'social benefits' of your car ownership. One obvious cost to society is that of producing the car. The price that your parents paid for the car may be an indication of that cost, although if the car company were being subsidized by the government and therefore the taxpayer, or the company were able to obtain raw materials such as oil at a much cheaper price than its long-run social cost, then the price paid for the car may differ from its actual or social cost.

But there are many other costs. There is the cost of roads, traffic lights, gritting in winter and all the others associated with the infrastructure needed to cope with the modern motor vehicle. There is the cost to other road users. You may be the cause of an accident: if you kill somebody, that is a cost to society. On a less important plane, your presence on the roads at key times of the day will slow down everybody else's progress. On one journey, for instance, you may cause 300 cars to be delayed by just 2 seconds on average. The total time lost is therefore 600 seconds or ten minutes. If we price everybody's time at just £1.80 an hour, you have cost society 30p in wasted time. Thirty pence is perhaps not a great deal, but if you commute to work, 2 journeys a day, 5 days a week, 45 weeks a year, that results in a cost to society of £135 (i.e. £0.30 × 2 × 5 × 45) a year.

The environmental costs should not be forgotten either. Your car will be a cause of pollution: there will be noise pollution; your exhaust fumes will give rise to air pollution. Much pollution may have been caused during the manufacture of the car—the environment may have been permanently damaged by mining the iron ore or coal necessary to build it, for instance. Roads, too, inflict damage on the environment: how many people seriously want to live next to a motorway?

The private cost of car ownership for you personally is very small, but the social costs are much greater. As to social benefits, the only benefit likely to accrue to society which is not a private benefit to you is that some of your friends and your family may have greater mobility themselves because you are willing either to drive them somewhere or let them use your car. At this stage, it is possible to see why it is probably not a good idea to give all young people a car. Although for the young person, the private benefits greatly outweigh the private costs, for society as a whole the social costs probably outweigh the social benefits.

Lowest cost

Most individuals or organizations consider only the private costs and benefits of their activities. A company, for instance, is likely to aim to be as competitive as possible. In part, that means producing at lowest cost. But 'lowest cost' means lowest cost for the firm, not necessarily lowest cost for society.

A firm may be able to cut costs by dumping untreated effluent into a local river or stream. Society must then accept the cost of suffering from or dealing with the effluent; the river may 'die' as a result of the dumping of effluent. Even if we put no price on the loss of quality of life of plants and animals which would otherwise have lived from the river, we should put a price on the loss of enjoyment of walkers, sightseers, anglers and boaters who will now be discouraged from enjoying this particular piece of nature. Downstream, businesses which were perhaps making use of water from the river will find the costs increased because they will either have to purify it or stop using it altogether. The local water authority may take water from the river as well as piping it to houses and factories. Extra pollution increases the water authority's costs.

Another example to show that 'lowest cost' is not necessarily best for society relates to safety. A firm may be able to cut costs by encouraging workers to ignore safety precautions in its factory: for instance, safety guards on a machine may slow down the rate of production. If a worker is on piece rates, he or she is likely to be tempted not to use the safety guards and management may be only too happy to turn a blind eye. The resulting injury of a worker may cost the firm next to nothing, but the social cost will be much greater. There will be the cost of medical treatment, and the suffering of the worker and his or her family. If the injury is serious enough, the worker may become physically handicapped and be a burden on society for the rest of his or her life.

Because individuals and organizations tend to consider only the private costs and benefits of their activities, it is essential that channels exist through which society as a whole can influence how individual economic agents behave. The obvious arbiter is the government. By passing laws and directing public spending and taxation, it can try to force individuals and firms to act as though they were considering all the costs and benefits of their actions instead of just their private ones. Most people would argue that Britain has become a better place to live in because governments have passed anti-pollution laws and laws which protect the consumer against unscrupulous firms.

However, because social costs and social benefits are hard to qualify, it is often difficult for a government to decide whether or not a particular economic activity is socially desirable. Would building five nuclear power stations be better for society than building five coal-fired power stations? Would building a new motorway from A to B benefit society overall? Should motorcyclists be forced to wear crash helmets? Should buses be subsidized? Should there be entrance fees to state museums and art galleries?

Exercise   What are the private costs and benefits to a motorcyclist of the legal requirement that crash helmets must be worn? What are the social costs and benefits?

Scarce resources

In Chapter 1, it was explained that the basic economic problem is that, because man lives in a world of finite (i.e. limited) resources, he has to choose between different bundles of economic goods and services. Land is one scarce factor of production. If land is used for a housing estate, it can't be used for agricultural purposes. If a factory is built on a piece of land, it can't be used as parkland. If a motorway is built through a beautiful piece of countryside, then the beauty of that countryside disappears.

There are many pressures on the environment today, because land is scarce and a number of different individuals and organizations want to use it for different purposes. If left to free market forces, much of the beauty of the British countryside would have been destroyed long ago. As it is, landowners who wish to build on their land normally have to obtain planning permission from local government. Much of the countryside is designated 'green belt' areas which means that it cannot be used for industrial or housing purposes. When new building is undertaken, in town or in the countryside, planning regulations limit what can be erected so that it will not destroy the character of a particular site. Mention has already been made of pollution controls, which limit the amount of pollution which businesses and individuals may create, and therefore limit the damage to the environment which economic activity generates.

But it is not only how scarce resources are allocated that is important. Decisions made today often have an impact on future generations. A decision to build a new town in the middle of the countryside not only deprives society of agricultural and recreational land today but will continue to do so for the foreseeable future. With something like a new town, the effects of the decision to build are fairly predictable.

This is not the case with, say, a nuclear power station. What will the cost be for future generations of dealing with radioactive waste, obsolete power stations and the pollution that a nuclear power station inevitably creates?

Take the case of non-renewable energy sources—like coal or oil. At current rates of exploitation, the world will run out of these forms of energy very quickly. By the year 3000, non-renewable energy could be a thing of the past. Oil could run out within your lifetime. The debate about whether or not the world needs to worry about these facts is a complex one. Some argue that there is no need to worry. As a raw material becomes scarcer, it rises in price. This directly reduces demand for the product and encourages industry to find more efficient processes for its use. On the other hand, known sources of the raw material may well increase, as man explores more and more areas of the world and, in the future, beyond this planet. In the early 1970s, for instance, there was much talk of an 'oil crisis', and people predicted that it might run out within a few decades. Yet, ten years later, with oil prices at a higher level, less oil is being consumed world-wide, while known reserves have increased.

But natural oil must run out sometime. There are those who argue that man's technology will not always be able to keep pace with shrinking natural resources. At some stage the economic world as we know it will collapse because man in the past has used up natural resources too fast. On this argument, conserving our resources and protecting our environment becomes all important, far too important to be left to the ups and downs of free market forces.

The debate about how best to use our natural resources and the environment is a vital one, and will be just as important if not more so in 50 years' time. The pressures on the environment are many and varied. Society as a whole must sort out these conflicting pressures and decide on what should be given priority. Scarcity means that man has to choose, and choice is difficult.

Exercise

It is predicted that Britain's coal reserves will run out by the year 3000. Should Britain use less coal now so that reserves will last longer? Explain your answer carefully.

Important points to keep in mind

1. **Man's economic activities have a decisive effect on the environment.**

2. **When judging whether or not man's activities are on the whole beneficial or harmful, it is necessary to consider all the benefits and costs to society of those activities. Economists call these the 'social benefits' and 'social costs'.**

3. **Individuals make their decisions considering only the private costs and benefits of the activities. Therefore, it is essential that government intervenes, through laws or economic policy, when these private costs and benefits differ widely from the social costs and benefits of an activity.**

4 Conservation policies are necessary when man is using up too many of the scarce resources of the planet at the expense of future generations.

Rash assault

£20m 'rash assault' on lake

By Michael Morris

A £20 million Arab investment for a leisure complex in the Lake District has put the developers and local people at loggerheads.

Residents claim that the proposed development at Bowness-on-Windermere, rising on seven levels to 80 feet, would dominate an otherwise rural and wooded scene at the lake's margin.

About 320 yards long, it would include a conference building, 264 apartments, parking for 1,211 cars, ice rink, swimming pool with wave pattern machine for surfboarding, indoor bowling, squash courts, saunas, restaurant and bar.

Speaking before a meeting tomorrow of South Lakeland district council, which will consider the project, Mr Jack Jones, the architect, said: 'It is going to lift the Lake District out of the late twentieth-century into the twenty-first century.'

But the proposal has aroused the anger of many in the region, including the Friends of the Lake District.

The Friends' secretary, Mr Mike Houston, said the leisure development was not related to the enjoyment of the Lake District's natural qualities.

Residents who formed a group to protect the site strongly attacked the proposed development at a public meeting as exploitation of one of the most superb sites in the Lake District and contrary to National Park policy.

Mr John Trotter told the meeting that 3,000 visitors a day (adding 1,000 cars to traffic congestion) would be needed in the summer to make the project a paying proposition.

Source: The Guardian, 22 April 1985

TASK

1 Describe the proposal put forward by Arab investors.

2 What would be the likely private benefits of this project to:

a   workers in the lake district
b   tourists
c   South Lakeland District Council?

3 What would be the likely private costs of the project to:

a   local residents
b   tourists?

4 Should the proposal be given planning approval? Explain your answer carefully.

Area survey

This project can be done on either an individual or a group basis.

TASK 1

Choose an area which you know well. You should be able to obtain a highly detailed map of the area (for instance, a small-scale ordnance survey map or an 'A to Z' street map), and be able to survey the area on foot or by bike. An area one mile square should be quite large enough.

TASK 2

Draw up a map of the area you have chosen. Mark on it all the roads, and the names of the main roads. Then shade in different colours the areas which are used for:

1 residential use, e.g. houses, flats

2 commercial use, e.g. shops, pubs, launderettes, estate agents

3 industrial use, e.g. factories

4 agricultural use, e.g. farming land

5 recreational use, e.g. parks, playing fields

6 community use, e.g. schools, fire stations, council offices

TASK 3

Consider the implications of a change in land use of **three** sites in your area.

a What would the social costs and benefits be if

  i a new factory making dangerous chemicals

  ii a hypermarket with large car park

  iii a large comprehensive school were built in the area you have chosen to survey.

b Where would you site these three developments?

Threat to green belt

Threat to build town on London green belt farms

By Geoff Andrews, Local Government Correspondent

Plans for a new town on farmland in the London green belt for 12,000 people will be followed by up to six more around the capital, the developers said yesterday.

The Development Consortium, a group of 10 of the largest housebuilding companies in the country, disclosed details of plans for the first town at West Horndon, Essex, on a 760-acre farm, between Basildon, Brentwood, Upminster and Grays. It made a formal planning application to Thurrock Council, which opposes the proposal.

The first new town is the first important sign of planning pressure on the green belt springing from the M25 London orbital motorway, four miles to the west.

The developers claim that while they regard the motorway as a boon they do not want to build a middle-class dormitory for commuters. They believe that they have the only solution to growing pressures on housing land in the South-east, where 40 per cent of the price of a new home is accounted for in the land value.

Mr David Lock, the consortium's project manager, said that the site was a flat and featureless field used for growing wheat and rape which was probably going into Common Market intervention stocks. This was an exceptional case which warranted breaking green belt rules.

'The green belt is an extraordinary planning achievement but it has been spread like a blanket around London and used as a defence mechanism by people living in great style in the countryside while people in London live in appalling conditions,' he said. Asked if this meant that the new town was planned for sale to such people, he said: 'It is not impossible.'

The planners are convinced that they can make the town a balanced community with a shopping centre, schools and health centre. There would be council houses and sheltered housing if the local authority agreed and they would like the town to have a parish council.

Source: The Guardian, 9 May 1985

1 What is the 'green belt'?

2 What has the Development Consortium proposed?

3 Why does the Development Consortium need to make a 'planning application' before starting the new town?

4 Why should the fact that a new motorway, the M25, has just been built make the site at West Hordon an attractive one to build a new town?

5 Why do the builders suggest that a new town is needed in the area?

6 What is the land presently used for?

7 What would be

  a the social benefits and
  b the social costs

  of building a new town at West Hordon as opposed to keeping it as a farm?

8 Why are the developers of the site so keen to build the new town?

9 Thurrock Council has to make a choice; either it allows the proposed development to go ahead or it keeps the land as farming land. What choice do you think it should make? Explain your answer carefully.

138

New fears as more Bhopal victims die

From Ajoy Bose in Bhopal

Union Carbide yesterday announced that it is giving nearly $1 million in aid for the Bhopal disaster victims. The poisonous gas leak in the central Indian city killed more than 2,500 people and put 125,000 in hospital.

In a statement issued several hours after the chemical giant's chairman, Mr Warren Anderson, had secretly left the country, Union Carbide also announced that it was setting up an orphanage in Bhopal.

The aid move was announced after the filing of a lawsuit in the US claiming $15 billion in damages from the company. The suit, filed in Charleston, West Virginia, on behalf of two Indians who lost a wife and a son as a result of the leak, alleges negligence in design and claims that the company failed to warn of the chemical's dangers.

Six days after the leak of the methyl isocyanate gas from the pesticide factory, people are still dying. Hospitals said that at least 50 more deaths had been reported in the past 24 hours and more than 100 new patients admitted to hospital.

Doctors at Bhopal's Hamidia Hospital said that the deaths were the result of the delayed effect of poisoning by the gas.

But, although the hospital is still getting a rush of patients, the superintendent, Dr N. R. Bhandari, feels that the worst is probably over.

There are, however, many secondary dangers. The appallingly poor hygienic conditions in affected areas have aroused fears that cholera and typhoid epidemics could break out.

Dr Bhandari, who said his hospital had so far treated 65,000 people, warned of the dangers resulting from poor nourishment.

Bodies are decomposing in makeshift graveyards, attracting thick swarms of flies. In one cemetery, bodies have started emerging from graves because they were dug too shallow. Health officials last night started to dig deeper graves.

The continuing deaths have spread panic in the city, despite assurances by authorities that the city's air is now safe and that meat, fish and poultry are uncontaminated.

The new fears have started a large-scale exodus from the town, with hundreds of people sending their families as far from Bhopal as possible.

In the city, the mood is slowly turning from grief to anger. One taxi driver, asked to go to the Union Carbide factory, said: 'Don't call it Union Carbide, call it Killer Carbide.'

Source: The Guardian, 10 December 1984

TASK

1 How many people were reported killed or injured in Bhopal?

2 What was the cause of the accident?

3 What was the name of the company which owned the factory?

4 What was produced at the factory?

5 What were the causes of death and illness in Bhopal?

6 When Union Carbide set up its factory in Bhopal, it was welcomed there. What were the social benefits of the factory to:

   a   Indian workers, particularly in Bhopal
   b   the city of Bhopal
   c   Indian farmers
   d   industry and commerce in Bhopal and the rest of India?

7 What have been the social costs of the Bhopal factory?

8 Have the social costs of the Bhopal factory been greater than its social benefits? Explain your answer.

9 What lessons does the Bhopal incident teach us about the need for pollution controls in the chemical industry?

Environmental issue   **139**

TASK

Take a local environmental issue. It could involve a new road scheme or problems with existing roads. Or it might be concerned with the industrial activity of a local firm. It might relate to a change in use of a local piece of land, from say woodland to housing land. Or it might be an issue centred on local wildlife. Describe the background to the issue. Explain the positions that various interested parties (landowners, residents, workers, factory owners, etc.) have taken up. Evaluate who is right by weighing up carefully all the social costs and social benefits involved in the issue. How do you think it will be resolved?

Farmers' greed

TASK

1 What is Prince Charles' complaint against British farmers?

2 Why is a change to 'organic farming' likely to lead to

a reduced environmental pollution
b healthier food in the shops
c reduced 'surpluses of just about every ... major commodity'
d higher prices for food in the shops?

3 Why is 'the greed of farmers' to blame for the loss of 'fascinating places, wetlands, moorlands and hedgerows'?

4 A farmer could grow an extra £1 000 worth of food if he or she uprooted a 600-yard hedgerow. Would it be worth it

a for the farmer and
b for the economy?

5 A farmer has been growing a species of plant unique to the British Isles in 5 acres of wetland (but it is found elsewhere in Europe in isolated spots). He is thinking of draining the wetland and using it for farming. What is the value of food which he or she would have to grow in the 5 acres for the economy as a whole to benefit from this?

Muck-spreader Charles lashes greedy farmers

By Ashley Walton

Prince Charles, angry over what he sees as the mutilation of the countryside, attacked the greed of farmers yesterday.

'We have come to look on the land as an endless source of increasing income without too much regard to the old conventional view of giving back to the land,' he said.

The Prince is switching his Gloucestershire acres to organic farming relying on good old-fashioned muck spreading rather than chemical fertilisers.

'Some of Britain's most beautiful countryside has been lost because of farmers' greed,' said the Prince.

He was speaking at a conference on future land use at Seale Hayne Agricultural College in Newton Abbot, Devon, in his capacity as the Duke of Cornwall—one of Britain's biggest landowners.

He said that 45 years of maximising production had led to butter mountains, milk lakes and surpluses of just about every other major commodity.

Greed

'Food surpluses have gained but the countryside and nation have been the losers,' he said.

'Fascinating places, wetlands, moorlands and hedgerows have been lost in response to greed.'

Already a committed vegetarian and follower of fringe medicine, the Prince is going right back to nature at his country estate, Highgrove in Gloucestershire.

Source: Daily Express, 4 April 1985

13 New technology

Technological advance

Modern civilization would never have been possible without technology. It was man's technological achievements which allowed *homo sapiens* to come to dominate the planet earth and partially control its environment.

There is much talk today of the 'new technologies'—computers and chips, biogenetics etc. Yet new technologies are nothing new to man. Specific periods of history are named after the new technologies of the time—like 'the bronze age' or 'the iron age'. Two hundred years ago, Britain experienced an 'Industrial Revolution'. A large number of inventions linked to discoveries about power generation combined to change the face of Britain over a 100-year period. Important technological changes have occurred since: the coming of the railway, the invention of the motor car, the use of gas and electricity, the telephone, television, plastics. What lessons can be learnt from the past? What will the 'new' technologies of today bring us in the future?

New products

One result of the new technology has been and will be new products. The micro chip has already had an important impact upon many traditional goods and services. Electric washing machines, new control panels in cars, and even electronic displays of the weather forecast on television are a few examples. Distinctly new products have emerged: video tape recorders, calculators and home computers, for instance. The world of the future will be an electronic world. What that might mean in practice can only be guessed at but at its heart will be major advances in 'information technology'. The television screen linked to a computer, telephone link, cable or satellite will become the centre of information gathering, control and entertainment for a household. Electronic shopping, control of domestic appliances like cookers, visual communication with persons at the other end of a telephone line and availability of financial services are all very likely to occur in the next 20 or 30 years in the average home.

The new products that will become the norm over the next few decades are likely to be commercially available already. In the 1930s, for instance, the 'necessities' of today, like television, refrigerators, telephones and motor cars, were already in existence, but only available in fairly primitive forms to the more well off in society. So, what are the luxury high technology goods of today that will rapidly become available in more advanced forms to the average citizen of the future?

Exercise

What new technology products have you got in your home? What advantages do they bring? What new technology products would you like to have but can't afford at the moment? Why would you like to have them?

Employment and unemployment

It's all very well looking forward to a bright electronic future, but new technology could impoverish millions of people. The reason is that new technology will not only result in new consumer products, but it will have a major impact on production processes. The new technology will allow the same number of goods and services to be produced with far fewer workers. Computers have already had a major impact, for instance, on the numbers of workers employed in financial services such as banking and building societies. Despite rapid growth in custom in recent years, banks and building societies have not taken on new workers because machines have been taking over much of the work previously done by employees. The UK manufacturing industry, with declining sales and the introduction of new technology, saw the disappearance of 2 million jobs in five years between 1979 and 1984.

Many have predicted that the new technologies will lead to mass unemployment; machines will replace workers. It is then argued that, while the fortunate few who have jobs will continue to improve their standard of living, the rest, the unemployed, will subsist in permanent poverty. The new technology will benefit some but leave the rest poorer than ever.

Others argue that this analysis is too simplistic. To begin with, jobs will be lost in traditional industries but fairly quickly new ones will be created in industries producing new technology products. Television manufacturers may shed workers as production lines are automated. Manufacturers of video-tape recorders, however, are likely to take on workers. Job losses may for a time exceed new jobs created, but in the long run technological unemployment should disappear.

Moreover, as those in work become more affluent, they will take part of their real wage increase in the form of reduced working hours: early retirement will become more and more common; the average number of hours worked per week will continue to fall; holiday entitlement will be increased. This will create job opportunities for the unemployed.

Looking to the past, it is clear that new technologies have not resulted in permanent mass unemployment, but there has been a very long history of people predicting the worst as one or other new labour-saving machine is introduced. Economies have always adjusted. That doesn't mean to say that the unemployment that new technology may bring for a 'short' while is nothing to be worried about. High unemployment in Britain is predicted to remain until at least 1990, which is a personal tragedy for everybody caught in the trap. With unemployment in millions, that adds up to millions of personal tragedies and an enormous cost to the country as a whole. Measures to alleviate technological unemployment should be given highest priority.

Exercise

Do you think 'new technologies' could make teachers redundant? Explain the reasons for your answer.

Technology and the environment

Technology can be seen as the enemy of the environment. Nuclear power stations, coal mines, factories belching forth pollution all destroy the environment. Technology, however, can also be a force for preserving the environment. As technology advances, it is possible to control man's damage to the environment without turning the clock back to a point where there were no factories or coal mines. Technology also gives society the resources to deal with damage to the environment. Far more is spent on environmental protection per unit of output in the rich industrialized high technology countries of the world than in poorer low technology Third World countries.

Exercise

Through reading the newspaper or listening to the television or radio, find out and write about one way in which new technology is helping protect the environment at the moment.

The standard of living

Will new technology improve the standard of living of the country or reduce it? To answer this question, we must make use of the concepts of social cost and social benefit. So long as all the benefits gained by society (the social benefits) are greater than all the costs (the social costs), then new technology has been beneficial. Some of the major benefits of new technology have already been mentioned: new products, higher incomes and reduced working hours are substantial benefits in themselves. Moreover, new technology will bring improved working conditions. Factories and offices will be cleaner, healthier and pleasanter places to work in. Many jobs involving repetitive tasks — such as production-line work or copy typing—will disappear as machines take them over. More interesting jobs, which require workers to perform a number of different, non-routine tasks, will be too expensive to automate and therefore will remain.

The costs are the unemployment costs—which, hopefully, will last only a relatively short time—and the possible dangers to our society that certain new technologies such as nuclear power bring in their wake. New technology can also fundamentally alter the way in which we live. Looking back 200 years in Britain, it is possible to see a land where the majority of people lived and worked in the countryside and where factories, housing estates and chemical works were either a rarity or not even known. Some argue that the average British citizen was better off living in this mainly rural environment. Man was close to nature and lived in a world where television, cinemas and discos had not yet destroyed the simpler pleasures of life. However, most people today would not take this view. Britain in the 1980s might have high unemployment, a crime problem, millions living in poverty and rampant vandalism. But at least virtually nobody dies of malnutrition or works an average 80 to 100 hours a week. Housing standards, life expectancy, diet and sanitation are all much improved. Besides unemployment, crime, poverty and vandalism were common in eighteenth-century Britain.

The benefits of technology are much dearer than the costs. But the social benefits are likely to exceed the social costs. After all, how many people today would want to live as an ordinary person in the 1930s or the 1880s or the 1780s?

Exercise

Name one 'new technology' product. What are the social costs and social benefits of this product? On balance, is it beneficial to society?

Work and leisure in the future

The average working week has declined over the past 200 years in Britain. In the nineteenth century, working 60 to 80 hours a week was normal. The Chartist demand in the 1830s and 1840s for a working week of just 40 hours was considered revolutionary. Even today, the average working week for full-time employees is still just over 40 hours, but that includes overtime. Over the 20-year period 1961 to 1981, average working hours fell 10%; so, by the year 2000, the average working week could be down to 36 or 37 hours and by the time you are nearing retirement, it may be down to 30 hours a week. Holiday entitlement will also increase from a norm of three to four weeks a year to perhaps five or six weeks.

Much has been written about the move to a 'leisure society'. One hundred years ago, the average worker spent his or her time working, eating and sleeping; he or she had very little time for leisure pursuits. In 100 years' time, the average worker is likely to spend only 15 or 20 hours a week working, and that for possibly only 30 years of his or her lifetime instead of the 45 years at present. That means that people will have a lot more time for themselves, to develop their own leisure pursuits. If the experience of the past 100 years is anything to go by, people choose leisure pursuits which involve the spending of money. That means that the average person unemployed, with little or no money to spare, and with a great amount of leisure time on his or her hands, will not be able to use that leisure time very constructively. A job which brings in income will be the passport to enjoyment of leisure in the future. This is one more reason why unemployment represents such a cost to the individuals concerned and therefore to society as a whole.

Important points to keep in mind

1. The 'new' technologies of today are the latest in a series of technological advances which man has experienced down the ages.

2. Major benefits of the new technologies will include new products, better working conditions and shorter hours of work.

3. In the short run—and that could be a period of ten or more years— new technology may cause unemployment as machines replace men, but in the longer term the economy should return to full employment.

Standard of life

This assignment will enable you to compare life as it was 50 years ago with life as it is today, and you can achieve it by conducting an interview with a retired person.

TASK 1

Draw up a questionnaire. You are to interview a retired person about life as he or she remembers it 50 years ago. The aim is to be able to compare the standard of living enjoyed 50 years ago with that enjoyed today. In particular, you should ask questions which relate to the advances made in technology and their impact on living standards over the period. Some of the questions to be asked might include:

Did you have a refrigerator in your home 50 years ago? How did you cope without one? What entertainment was there before television? Was life better without television? How long did people work compared to today? What were working conditions like compared to today? Has the motor car, with all its noise and pollution, improved life over the past years?

TASK 2

Decide on whom you will interview. The interviewee should be a retired person over 65 years old. You might ask one of your relatives or a neighbour. Fix a time and a place for the interview. Record the answers on paper during the interview. Do not be afraid to ask questions other than those you have already written down if you feel it is necessary. You may prefer to tape the interview, but you must ask permission of the interviewee first.

TASK 3

Write a 1000-word report based on your interview. The title of the report is: 'How technology and living standards have changed over the past 50 years.'

Robot nurse

Enter a robot nurse

By John Newell

It's the little things that get you down, particularly if you're disabled. The humiliating need to have help with simple tasks such as bathing and eating is a continual battering to the spirit.

Now American research could bring robots into the ward - and even into the wheelchair - and give the disabled more

control over their own lives by doing away with the necessity for human attendants.

A team led by Dr Larry Leifer at the American Rehabilitation Research and Development Centre at Palo Alto, California, has used microelectrics and new work in production line robotics to develop the 'mechanical orderly'.

The robot has an arm with shoulder, elbow, wrist and finger joints controlled through 12 separate microcomputers by a combination of spoken commands and head movements. The arm ends in a 'smart' hand with two or three fingers and 12 electronic eyes, optical sensors which measure the distance of the fingers from whatever they are being told to grip.

A second version now being developed has touch sensors which act like cats' whiskers, gauging distances by lightly brushing surfaces.

Eventually the robot could be trained to bathe, feed and groom patients, particularly paraplegics. Spoken commands tell the robot which of its tasks to perform, and detailed guidance is given by slight movements of the head.

The research team has also developed the 'smart' wheelchair, again controlled by slight movements of the head but also capable of controlling its own movements.

Source: The Sunday Times, 17 March 1985

TASK

1 In your own words, describe the 'robot nurse' outlined in the article.

2 In what ways will this 'robot nurse' help disabled people?

3 Why do you think relatively few 'robot nurses' will be provided to disabled people in the immediate future?

4 Describe some of the other tasks round the home that a 'mechanical orderly' robot might be able to do.

5 If 'mechanical orderlies' cost the same as a small car, do you think that they would be commonplace in homes? Give reasons for your answer.

You've never had it so good!

Why we've never had it so good

By Anthony Eccles

Racked by unemployment and bearing the consequences of recession, it is hard for us to realise how fortunate we are.

Yet the thought occurred while I was being driven briskly through country lanes by my father, as he chattered about laser surgery and interactive videodiscs. He was born in 1899.

In his lifetime he has seen a transformation in the conditions of the better off inhabitants of this planet; an improvement faster and more radical than any comparable period in history.

Yet, in 1899, no aeroplane had yet flown properly, though a balloon had crossed the Channel more than a century earlier. Quantum theory had yet to evolve, Einstein's theory of relativity was unpublished, medicines were ill-developed and housing for the poor was truly frightful. Much had happened of course. Mechanical reapers were used in fields, where steam engines occasionally supplemented the horses. The electric telegraph and transcontinental railways existed, as Western films demonstrate.

Tuberculosis and diphtheria were still menacing. As like as not, an aching tooth would just be pulled out, without anaesthetic, by the local chemist. Diet was monotonous and knowledge of vitamins and nutrition as yet crude. There were still some two million domestic servants in Britain — partly providing security, but mainly to engage in the laborious drudgery of clothes beating, fire laying and endless cleaning. We do not 'spring clean' now — except as a ritual — for our houses stay clean. Those servants were needed as the strengthening sunlight revealed the grime of winter's coal smoke. Bronchial fogs were common in cities — even up to the 1950s.

The early motor cars — often electric in New York — were hailed as major eliminators of pollution, for town streets, some unmetalled, were thick with horse manure over which one had to pick one's way to the horse tram, let alone to the other side.

Those servants were kept busy, but it is interesting to consider their social position when you look at Victorian and Edwardian houses. They lived in attics and cellars, connected by more than one staircase in the grandest houses. So how could the family have much privacy to quarrel, to make love, to feel free — except by assuming that their servants didn't really

147

count, that what they thought or said was of no consequence?

Marconi had spanned the Atlantic with the wireless in 1901, while refrigerated ships were providing fresher meat from Australia and Argentina. Although gas lighting was still common and remained so in the streets until after the second world war, by 1914 the motor bus was widely in use and commuting crowds were long familiar.

The first world war — which probably would not have lasted a year if today's television journalism had been available — saw the invention of the tank. Who recalls now, as we worry about police power and the miners that, in 1919, we were to have tanks on the streets during Liverpool's police strike?

Washing and changing of clothes was relatively infrequent, though the professional classes often changed their grimy collars daily, if not their shirts. Even in 1951, 45 per cent of households lacked a fixed bathtub. Under 5 per cent had a refrigerator or a washing machine. Less than half of homes had a vacuum cleaner.

The thirties had produced television, the jet engine, penicillin, the splitting of the atom and Keynesian economics. Consumer goods were falling in price as assembly lines cut the costs of manufacture.

The forties were to offer the nuclear reactor, electronic computer and the solid-state transistor, later to become the 'chip.' Central heating was still unusual, despite the Romans having pioneered it some 2000 years earlier. The anxiety-reducing contraceptive pill was on its way in the fifties and the first Sputnik took off in 1957.

Awe-inspiring complexities of genetic codes were being unlocked by work on DNA molecules and the electronics industry was already embarked on its quest for amazing enhancements of miniaturisation, speed and power. To discuss the advances in epidemiology, surgery and chemotherapy would take an article in itself.

People are beginning to eat and to live healthier lives and are developing a healthy scepticism of the scientist or doctor as God. Even natural foods are no longer automatically assumed to be beneficial and, as for food variety, not only do we expect variety and freshness meal to meal, some families expect choices person by person within each meal. Social understanding — be it about sexuality or abnormal behaviour — has grown markedly more sophisticated; the complexities of sub-atomic particles and astro-physics are little short of stunning.

The position of women in society has generally improved while much adult laughter about childrens' computer capabilities has an envious ring about it. We now expect to be present, via colour television, at every important world news, entertainment and sporting event. From increasingly accurate weather forecasting, better crop yields, non-invasive diagnosis from magnetic resonance imaging, fibre optics to show us the insides of previously impenetrable surroundings, the list of advances is breathtaking. It is a panorama from quill pen to laser printer in a lifetime.

It is true that we have lots of unfinished tasks. And we constantly inspire ourselves to seek new goals. The coincidence of high unemployment and the grim inadequacy of social supports for the disadvantaged is a failure of our ability to govern and motivate ourselves. We are still improving houses built to the minimum by-law standards of the 1890s. The growth in mobility of the affluent has not been matched for the poor who are dependent on public transport. It is not clear that standards of honour in public life are improving greatly. Commercial greed can still present an unedifying spectacle. Crime seems to have lapsed back towards 19th century levels — those Victorian window shutters and grilles weren't there just for decoration.

However, some more advances are nearly upon us. The understanding and treatment of some currently fatal diseases is close. The act of smoking will soon achieve its deserved status on a par with spitting.

And whilst we castigate the failures of housing policies, it is worth remembering that even 'hard to let' council properties often have adequate weather proofing, hot and cold running water, electricity, central heating and indoor flushing toilets. Most families now own their own homes, compared with less than 10 per cent in 1900, and today these homes usually contain more equipment than a turn of the century factory. Further improvement in communications, transport, health and housing are obviously attainable. Were they really the good old days?

Source: The Guardian, 25 February 1985

Personal experience

TASK

1 Describe the following aspects of life of a typical servant in 1899:

   a medical health
   b work undertaken
   c living conditions
   d diet
   e entertainment
   f washing and changing of clothes
   g threat from criminal activity
   h transport.

2 Make a list of all the developments which have taken place this century mentioned in the article.

3 Take **two** of these developments and explain how they have improved the standard of living of the ordinary person.

4 Pick another **two** of these developments and explain how they have caused a reduction in the standard of living of the ordinary person.

5 Some argue that we were better off 100 or 200 years ago. Do you think this is true? *Explain your answer carefully.*

6 In 50 years' time, you will be a retired person. You may look back to today and call the 1980s 'the good old days'. In what ways do you think that the average person will be better off or worse off in 50 years' time?

149

TASK

Identify new technology which you have experienced over the past two years at home, at school or anywhere else in your environment. Describe the nature of the new technology. Examine its impact upon yourself and those you live, work and recreate with. Discuss the extent to which you think this new technology has improved your standard of living.

14 Britain and the world

150 **Inter-dependence**

'I stand on my own two feet. I don't depend on anyone.' Have you ever heard someone say this? Many people like to think that they are independent and don't rely on others. But, in fact, virtually nobody is totally independent, and certainly not economically so.

This is because the British economy and the world economy is based upon **specialization**. An individual worker, a company, a nation specializes in producing a particular good or service, which is sold for money. With that money, other goods and services are bought. The great advantage of specialization is that a group of workers can produce far more goods and services by working together and co-operating than if they were to work as individuals.

Imagine what it would be like if everybody tried to be economically independent. There would be no shops to buy anything from. There would be no sophisticated technological goods, such as cookers, television or cars, because these can only be produced by complex organizations utilizing the skills of many different workers. There would be no electricity or gas or clean piped water. Everybody would be involved in a desperate struggle for survival, trying to grow enough food for themselves to eat, collecting fuel for heating and cooking, and maintaining or building shelters. Many would die within a short time as diseases carried by unclean water or unsanitary conditions in homes would spread rapidly. Indeed, many people would have to die because this planet could not feed its present population without the help of machinery such as tractors, fertilizers and high-yielding seeds and animal stock.

Individuals need other individuals to survive, and the same is true today of countries. Foreign trade has grown to such an extent that Britain's exports and imports account for nearly 40% of total production in this country. Britain buys from abroad to obtain goods and services which are either not produced in this country or are produced more cheaply abroad. If Britain were to stop exporting and importing tomorrow, the economy would collapse. Millions would lose their jobs and living standards for those in work would decline dramatically.

So we live in an economic environment where everybody is economically interdependent. Let us now consider in more detail the economic links between Britain and the rest of the world.

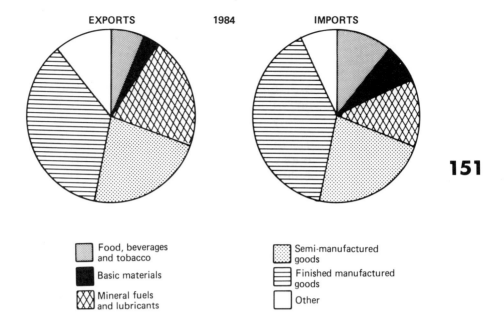

EXPORTS   1984   IMPORTS

151

Food, beverages
and tobacco

Basic materials

Mineral fuels
and lubricants

Semi-manufactured
goods

Finished manufactured
goods

Other

Exercise

Make a list of the goods and services which you and the household
you live in produce and which you yourselves consume. Make a
second list of goods and services which you buy from others. To
what extent are you economically independent of others?

**Exports and
imports**

Britain sells goods and services to foreigners: these are called
exports. We also buy goods and services from foreigners: these
are called **imports**. The two pie charts show what types of goods
Britain exported and imported. It can be seen that our biggest
single export and import was manufactured goods, such as cars,
nuts and bolts or machinery. Basic materials are raw materials
such as iron ore and copper that are needed to make
manufactured goods such as steel and cars. Fuels such as coal
and oil account for a significant proportion of exports and imports.
Before the days of North Sea oil, Britain exported very little fuel
but today much of North Sea oil production is sold abroad. The
other major category is food, drink and tobacco. Britain does not
grow enough food to feed its population, and part of what it grows
or manufactures is exported anyway. So food etc. has to be
imported.

Britain not only exports and imports goods but it also trades in
services. Foreign tourists visit Britain and spend money here while
British tourists travel abroad. Foreigners use banking, insurance

and other financial services, mainly in London, on which British firms make a profit. Similarly, British firms and citizens use foreign financial services for which they have to pay. Hiring ships and planes, and maintaining armies and embassies abroad are other examples of traded services. Finally, individuals, firms and governments borrow and lend money abroad on which they gain or pay interest, profits and dividends.

The difference between what Britain sells abroad—her exports—and what she buys abroad—her imports—is known as the **current balance** on the balance of payments. This is the figure that is often quoted in the news and is sometimes called simply the **balance of payments**. If the balance of payments on current account is in deficit, it means that the value of imports is larger than exports; if it is in surplus, it means that the value of exports is greater than the value of imports.

Surpluses and deficits on the current account are very important for Britain, which is why they are reported regularly in the news. If Britain has a deficit, it means that she has to borrow money or run down her foreign savings to pay for those exports. This is possible in the short run, but Britain cannot go on borrowing for ever. Britain as a nation is no different from you as an individual: eventually the bankers and governments who have lent her money will want to have it repaid with interest. The only way that this can be done is for Britain to start generating surpluses on its current account, exporting more than she imports, and using the surplus money to pay off its deficits. So, deficits are generally considered to be bad for Britain while surpluses are generally considered to be good.

Exercise

Make a list of all the products which you buy or have bought which are foreign-made. Why do you buy imported goods rather than British-made goods?

The capital account

It has already been mentioned that Britain borrows and lends money abroad. It is important to realize that most of this is done not by the government but by ordinary firms and citizens. Britain's borrowing and lending over a year is made up of millions of individual transactions. Because this is so, it is unlikely that in any one year, Britain's outflow of money for this purpose will exactly equal inflow.

Britain 'borrows' money for a variety of reasons. Firstly, foreigners might wish to invest directly in British industry. A Japanese car company might want to build a factory in Britain and so transfer money from Japan to Britain. Or an American company might buy shares in a British company, transferring money from the USA to the UK. Secondly, a British firm may want to borrow money from abroad to pay for imports or finance a project abroad. Thirdly, money may come into Britain for speculative purposes—more of this below. Similarly, money flows out of Britain as British companies invest abroad and lend money to foreign companies and governments.

Since the late 1970s, more money has flowed out of Britain for investment purposes than has come in. This can partly be explained by the fact that Britain now exports more than she imports due to North Sea oil. There is much controversy about whether or not this is a good thing for Britain.

On the one hand, Britain investing money abroad is rather like a person saving money. The investment builds up a nest-egg which can be used in the future to pay for imports and, more importantly, it will give a future income to Britain in the form of interest, profits and dividends earned abroad. On the other hand, money that flows abroad could have been invested in Britain. British firms could have used that money to buy factories, machines and offices which would have created jobs and raised incomes. It is difficult to say which is the better alternative because it is impossible to predict how good a particular investment will be. It could be that foreign investments will do very well in the future while British industry does very badly, even with extra investment; in that case, it would be better to invest abroad. On the other hand, foreign investments might do badly while British industry did well; investing at home would then make sense. At the moment, the government encourages British firms and individuals to invest abroad rather than keep the money here in Britain. Only time will tell whether the government is right.

Exercise

Which companies with premises in your local area are foreign owned? Make a list of a further ten companies operating in Britain which are foreign owned. What are the advantages and disadvantages to local people of having a foreign-owned company at work in the locality?

Exchange rates

Changes in the exchange rate are regularly announced on the news. Phrases like 'the pound went up today against the dollar' or 'the pound fell against the deutschemark today' are commonplace. But what does it all mean? Why do exchange rates change and is it important anyway?

The **exchange rate** is the value of one currency against another. If the exchange rate today were £1 to £10 French francs, then anybody wanting to buy French francs with pounds would have to pay £1 for 10 francs. Similarly, if the exchange rate were £1 to $2, then an individual wanting to buy, say, $200 would have to pay £100 for them.

There are a number of reasons why individuals, organizations and governments want to buy and sell foreign currencies. One very important reason is that foreign currency is needed to pay for imports of goods and services. Take the purchase by a British motorist of a Toyota car, manufactured in Japan. The Japanese company Toyota is unlikely to want British pounds in exchange for the car. They want Japanese money—Japanese yen—to pay their workers, buy materials, invest in new machinery, etc. in Japan. So Toyota in Japan sells cars to Toyota in Britain which in turn sells cars to garages which finally sell to the motorist. The motorist pays for his or her car in pounds. Toyota will sell those pounds for Japanese yen on what is called the **foreign exchange market**. It will sell to somebody who wants to buy pounds in exchange for Japanese yen—a Japanese company importing Scotch whisky.

A second important reason why foreign currency is bought and sold is that money is saved, invested and borrowed between countries. If an American company wants to set up a company in Britain, it will need to buy (or demand) pounds in exchange for US dollars. If a British citizen wants to buy shares in an American company, he or she would need to sell (or supply) pounds and buy (or demand) US dollars.

The rate of exchange, or the price of one currency against the other currencies, is fixed by the strength of demand and supply. The market for foreign exchange is no different from the market for, say, tomatoes. If there are a great many tomatoes to sell and few buyers around, prices will have to be low if they are all to be sold. On the other hand, if tomatoes are in short supply and many housewives want to buy (or demand) them, then prices will be high. So too with foreign exchange: if demand is high for a currency relative to its supply, then its price will tend to rise. If there are few buyers relative to sellers, prices will have to fall.

The rate of the pound against other currencies is important for Britain. If the value of the pound goes up against other currencies, imports become cheaper and exports become more expensive. For example, say the value of the pound rises from £1 = $1 to £1 = $2. An American company exporting computers from the USA to Britain would find it much easier to sell them because whereas previously a $10 000 computer would have sold for £10 000, its price at the new rate of exchange of £1 = $2 would be a mere £5 000. A high pound means more imports at a cheaper price for the British consumer. Cheap prices are good for the consumer but bad for British firms trying to sell their own products in Britain.

If the value of the pound falls, the reverse is true. Foreigners find that British goods are less expensive than before and therefore buy more of them. That should be good for British industry. On the other hand, British consumers have to pay higher prices for foreign goods. They're also likely to pay more for 'British' goods because most of them are made with imported raw materials or components. All this adds up to higher inflation in the British economy; and rising prices may swallow up the competitive advantage which British firms enjoyed as a result of a fall or **devaluation** of the pound. So changes in the value of the pound are important for prices and jobs in Britain.

Exercise

Using a local or national daily paper, plot the value of the pound against the dollar and one other currency (e.g. the French franc) for the next seven days. Try to give at least one reason why the value has changed over the period.

Important points to keep in mind

1. **Nobody in Britain is economically independent. People rely upon others to provide them with most of the goods and services consumed. This interdependence arises from specialization. Through specialization, the economy can produce far more goods and services than if everybody tried to work independently. Britain and the rest of the world are economically interdependent.**

2. **In part, this interdependence consists of trade in goods (visible trade) and services (invisible trade). The difference between the value of exports and the value of imports is known as the current balance.**

3. **In part, this interdependence consists of transfers of monies for saving, borrowing and investment.**

4. **The value of foreign trade is affected by the rate of exchange of the pound for foreign currency. The rate of exchange is fixed by the forces of demand and supply for the currency. A rise in the exchange rate, in the short term at least, should be good for prices, but bad for jobs. A fall should lead to a rise in prices in Britain but also an increase in the number of jobs available.**

Buy British?

The UK imports billions of pounds of produce each year. This assignment asks you to examine just how much of what you own is of foreign manufacture.

TASK

♦ Make a list of all the items you possess which were produced abroad.

♦ With your parents' permission, check in your kitchen cupboards/larder and write down all the canned/preserved food produce which has come from abroad.

♦ Which of your parents' large possessions (car, television, fridge, etc.) are foreign?

♦ Have you ever taken a foreign holiday? If so, where?

♦ Make a rough estimate of how much you personally spend on goods and services which are imported.

156

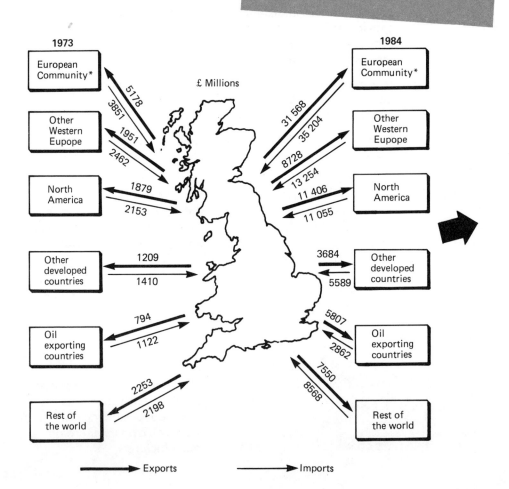

Visible trade by area

£ Millions

1973

European Community*
5178
3851

Other Western Euope
1951
2462

North America
1879
2153

Other developed countries
1209
1410

Oil exporting countries
794
1122

Rest of the world
2253
2198

1984

European Community*
31 568
35 204

Other Western Euope
8728
13 254

North America
11 406
11 055

Other developed countries
3684
5589

Oil exporting countries
5807
2862

Rest of the world
7550
8568

→ Exports   → Imports

	£millions			
	1973		1984	
	Exports	Imports	Exports	Imports
European community*	3 851	5 178	31 568	35 204
Other Western Europe	1 951	2 462	8 728	13 254
North America	1 879	2 153	11 406	11 055
Other developed countries	1 209	1 410	3 684	5 589
Oil exporting countries	794	1 122	5 807	2 862
Rest of world	2 253	2 198	7 550	8 568
Total	11 937	14 523	70 511	78 705

* Figures refer to the ten member countries in 1984. The UK joined the European Community in 1973.

Source: CSO, *Monthly Digest of Statistics*, No. 471; CSO, *United Kingdom Balance of Payments*, 1984

TASK

1 Which group of countries was our major trading partner in (*a*) 1973 and (*b*) 1984?

2 Estimate the percentage of total exports sold to (*a*) North America in 1973, (*b*) the rest of the world in 1973, (*c*) the European Community in 1984 and (*d*) oil-exporting countries in 1984.

3 Which export market has seen (*a*) the fastest growth and (*b*) the slowest growth for the UK over the period 1973 to 1984?

4 What was the balance of trade (i.e. exports minus imports) for the UK with (*a*) North America in 1973, (*b*) the European Community in 1984, (*c*) oil-exporting countries in 1984 and (*d*) the rest of the world in 1984?

5 Draw two pie charts, one for UK exports in 1973 and the other for UK exports in 1984.

6 Describe how the trade of the UK has changed over the period 1973 to 1984.

7 Give **two** reasons why this change has occurred.

Visible trade by commodity

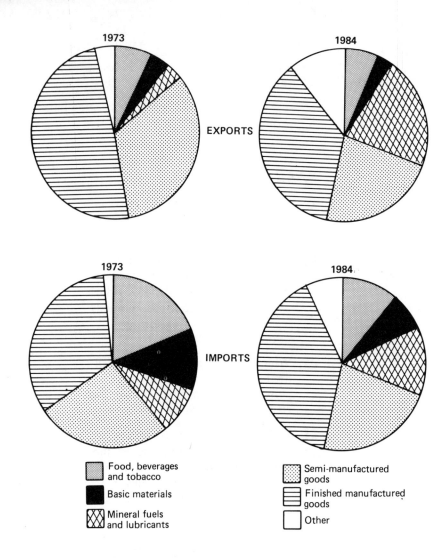

1973   1984   EXPORTS

1973   1984   IMPORTS

Food, beverages and tobacco

Basic materials

Mineral fuels and lubricants

Semi-manufactured goods

Finished manufactured goods

Other

Source: CSO, *Monthly Digest of Statistics,* No. 471; CSO, *United Kingdom Balance of Payments,* 1984

TASK

1. Give **two** examples of goods which would be classified as (a) food, beverages and tobacco, (b) basic materials, (c) mineral fuels and lubricants, (d) semi-manufactured goods and (e) finished manufactured goods.

2. Describe how (a) exports and (b) imports have changed over the period 1973 to 1984.

3. Estimate the value in £million of (a) exports of finished manufactured goods in 1973, (b) imports of semi-manufactured goods in 1973, (c) exports of mineral fuels and lubricants in 1984 and (d) imports of food, beverages and tobacco in 1984.

4. Over the period 1973 to 1984, why do you think that there has been (a) a very large increase in exports of mineral fuels and lubricants; (b) a percentage fall in exports and rise in imports of finished manufactured goods; (c) a substantial percentage fall in the imports of basic materials?

Hitachi to assemble VCRs at Hirwaun

Jurek Martin and Guy De Jonquieres in Tokyo

Hitachi, one of Japan's leading electronics groups, is to start assembling 5,000 video cassette recorders a month in July at its colour television factory at Hirwaun, South Wales.

The line, assembling imported kits, will be Hitachi's first in the UK and second in the EEC. It assembles VCRs in West Germany.

The company is prepared to consider complete manufacture in the UK in two to three years, depending on demand.

The £1m investment, which will provide a capacity of 10,000 units a month, will not create jobs initially, Hitachi emphasised in Tokyo yesterday. However, it will remove any threat of redundancies at Hirwaun.

The plant employs 800 people — a workforce which the current production of 25,000 colour televisions a month could not justify, Hitachi implied. Probably 100 jobs could have been at risk.

Source: Financial Times, 8 March 1985

TASK

1 What does Hitachi make?

2 Explain in your own words Hitachi's plans for its factory in Wales.

3 Why was Hitachi considering sacking 100 workers at its Welsh factory?

4 How much money will Hitachi invest at Hirwaun?

5 If 100 jobs are created, what is the cost per job of Hitachi's plans.

6 Should Britain encourage more Japanese manufacturers to set up here? In your answer, consider the effects on jobs, on other companies already established in Britain, on exports and imports and on consumers.

7 It costs the government over £5 000 a year to keep the average unemployed person on the dole. Would the money be better spent on creating workplaces like those at Hirwaun? Justify your answer. Why does the government not do this at present?

Export order

Clyde wins U.S. rig order

By Ian Hargreaves and Mark Meredith

UIE, the Clydebank rig-builder, has won a $60m (£50m) U.S. order to build the biggest drilling rig ever constructed in a UK yard. The order is from Transworld Drilling, a subsidiary of Kerr McGee.

This rare export order for the UK industry will secure the jobs of UIE's 500 permanent workers and create 500 more jobs when work on the rig reaches a peak.

Won against competition from Singapore, the order reflects the growing price-competitiveness of UK heavy offshore engineering companies as a result of the decline in sterling.

The order, for a so-called Gorilla class jack-up rig, is also a boost for Bouygues Offshore, which took over UIE (UK) this summer.

Bouygues Offshore is owned by Elf, the French oil company (34 per cent) and by the Paris-based Bouygues engineering and construction group (66 per cent). It is thought to have ambitious plans for expansion in the UK.

UIE hopes to win a substantial share of the work for the Elf-Total development of North Alwyn Field. Contracts are expected to be awarded soon.

The rig, which Transworld is building on a speculative basis, is due for delivery in June 1986. More than 14,000 tonnes of steel will be used in its construction. It will be capable of operating in water 300 ft deep. It will be convertible for use as a production platform.

Mr James Blackwood, the trade union spokesman at UIE, said they had written to Mr Paul Romano, Transworld's president, promising the unions would 'strive their utmost' to maintain the 12-year non-strike record.

Source: Financial Times, 13 December 1984

TASK

1. What has UIE won an export order for?

2. Give **two** reasons why Transworld Drilling placed the order with UIE.

3. What will be the possible effects of the order on jobs:

   a at UIE's Clydebank shipyard
   b at British Steel
   c in the area of Clydebank?

4. Why will the order help UIE to win more export orders from companies such as Elf–Total?

Britain's wealth abroad

TASK

1. What do you think is meant by 'Britain's wealth abroad'?

2. Calculate the number of working people in Britain.

3. The total population of the UK is 56 million. What is the average value of Britain's wealth for each person in 1983?

4. By how much has Britain's wealth increased over the period 1979 to 1983?

5. Why has Britain been able to invest so much abroad?

6. What do trade unions say should have happened to the money invested abroad?

7. What is the government agreement about investing money abroad?

8. What do you think should have been done with the money? Explain your answer carefully.

161

UK's overseas assets record

By Victor Keegan

Britain's wealth abroad climbed 15 per cent last year to a record £55.6 billion, according to Bank of England figures released yesterday. This is equivalent to about £2,600 for every working person.

Since 1979, net assets overseas have risen fourfold from £13 billion to £55.6 billion.

The build-up of assets abroad while unemployment in the UK has been reaching new records has often been criticised by the unions. It has happened as a result of government policy which was to remove restrictions on investment abroad in order to build up income-earning assets abroad against the day when North Sea oil runs out.

The government also argues that if there had not been such a strong outflow of funds, the pound would have been even stronger than it was, with the result that UK industry would have been even more uncompetitive.

The unions argue that more of this cash—much of which is their own pension fund money—should have been invested in the UK which suffered a 40 per cent decline in the volume of manufacturing investment during the recession.

Source: The Guardian, 29 June 1984

162

Ten split over imposing import quotas on Bangladesh

Alain Cass, *Asia Editor*

The EEC is split over whether to impose import quotas on Bangladesh. As one of the world's poorest nations, Bangladesh has been struggling to establish export industries in its bid for economic development.

The situation has arisen as a result of a massive increase in the imports of cheap shirts from Bangladesh into Britain, France and Germany in the past two years.

Although the amounts involved are relatively small — Bangladesh's share of total EEC garment imports totals less than 0.1 per cent in volume — the issues raised by the row highlight the problems of encouraging least developed countries (LDCs) to stand on their own feet and rely less on western aid.

Britain and France are behind the move to impose quotas on shirts from Bangladesh. Imports into Britain have soared from 200,000 in 1983 to over 1.2m last year. France is faced with increases of the same magnitude.

However, West Germany which last year imported 1.7m shirts from Bangladesh is opposed to imposing import quotas.

Bangladesh is arguing strongly that the imposition of quotas could cause massive unemployment in a new industry which employs 50,000 workers — 90 per cent of whom are women — and which already accounts for over 8 per cent of the country's export earnings.

The number of workers is expected to triple by the middle of this year. A major cut could in turn unleash serious social unrest, officials claim.

Moreover, Bangladesh officials argue, the industry is entirely funded by the private sector. One Bangladesh official said:

'First the West asks us to stand on our two feet by promoting profitable private industrial development. When we do just that they complain.'

Source: Financial Times, 5 February 1985

TASK

1. What do the initials 'EEC' stand for?

2. Name **three** member countries of the EEC.

3. What is an 'import quota'?

4. Explain why Britain, France and Germany are considering imposing import quotas on shirts from Bangladesh.

5. What would be the effect of imposing these import quotas on:

   a   jobs in Britain and Bangladesh
   b   the prices of shirts in Britain
   c   exports and imports in Britain and Bangladesh
   d   living standards in Britain and Bangladesh?

6. Why does industrial development in poorer countries of the world affect richer countries?

7. Do you think that the German position or the British and French position on the proposed import quotas is the correct one to take? Explain your answer carefully.

Car exports

Jaguar car exports boosted in 1984 by strength of the dollar

Kenneth Gooding *Motor Industry Correspondent*

Exports of Jaguar cars reached a record 25,880 in 1984 worth about £500m at existing showroom prices, the company said yesterday. This compared with 1983 exports of 22,141 cars worth around £420m.

The figures suggest that Jaguar's contribution to the UK balance of payments last year was roughly £400m, up from about £300m in 1983.

Jaguar is a major beneficiary from the strength of the U.S. dollar, since more than half of its total sales are made in the U.S.— its biggest individual market by far. The company is now the major UK exporter to the U.S. and the value of its cars is even greater than all the Scotch whisky shipped out to the U.S.

Last year, a record 18,044 Jaguar cars were sold in the U.S., up by 14 per cent from 15,815 in 1983. And 1984 ended more strongly than ever. December was the company's best-ever sales month in the States. For the first time, Jaguar sales topped 2,000 in one month, totalling 2,139.

However, the company insisted that it was not deliberately milking the U.S. markets for the high profits now available there. The percentage of total Jaguar car sales recorded in the States remained almost constant: 54 per cent last year against 54.2 per cent in 1983.

Source: Financial Times, 21 January 1985

TASK

1 What is an 'export'?

2 How many cars did Jaguar export in 1984? What was the total value of these exports? Estimate the average price of each car sold.

3 The article says that the dollar was strong in 1984. What does this mean?

4 *a* Assume that the value of the pound was £1 = $1.50. How much would a £20 000 Jaguar car sell for in dollars in the United States?

b Assume now that the value of the pound declined to £1 = $1. How much could a £20 000 Jaguar car now sell for in the United States?

c Would Jaguar be likely to sell more or fewer cars after the fall in the value of the pound?

5 The article says that 'high profits' are 'now available' in the United States. Why should profit on a car increase for Jaguar if the company decided to continue selling cars for £40 000 on average even though the value of the dollar increased from £1 = $1.50 to £1 = $1?

6 What effect did a strong dollar have on jobs in Britain?